Creating a Lifestyle You Can Live With

RON L. FRONK, PH.D.

Creating a
Lifestyle

YOU CAN

Live With

Creating A Lifestyle You Can Live With

Ron L. Fronk

Copyright © 1988 by Ron L. Fronk
Printed in the United States of America
ISBN:0-88368-202-8

Edited by David L. Young

Unless otherwise noted, Scripture quotations are taken from the *New American Standard Bible,* copyright © The Lockman Foundation, 1960, 1962, 1963, 1968, 1971, 1972, 1973, 1975, 1977 and used by permission.
Scripture quotations marked NIV are taken from the *New International Version* copyright © 1973, 1978, 1984, International Bible Society and used by permission.

This book is dedicated to people like you who have a sincere desire to consistently do your best, to become all that you can become, and who want to help others do the same.

Appreciations

Thank you to my wife, Susan, for your typing, your editing, and your ideas; for your patience, your motivation, and your love. You are an inspiration and truly my best friend.

Thank you, Mom, for trying to protect me and yet encouraging me to become all I could be.

Thank you for telling the truth, with the exception of the Easter Bunny, the Tooth Fairy, and Santa Claus.

Thank you for reminding me that I would have to do my own laundry if I ran away from home.

Thank you for loving me enough to discipline me.

Thank you for your advice, such as, "put clean socks and underwear on in case you get into an accident and have to go to the doctor" and "don't pick at it or it won't heal."

Thank you for nursing me through the coughs, the colds, the measles, the mumps, and the chicken pox; and heaven forbid that we forget the scrapes, the stitches, the scars, the burns, and the broken bones.

Thank you for your counseling during the trials, tribulations, tears of puppy love, and just plain growing up.

Thank you for providing stability during the storms of family life; the Lord knows there were many.

Thank you for understanding when I didn't realize that you, too, had a life to live.

Thank you to my father. He taught me much more than he ever realized.

Thank you to my favorite brother, Gary, for always being very supportive and a friend through the good times and the bad.

Thank you to my favorite sister, Diana, for impacting me with your wonderful attitude and love.

Thank you to my favorite sister, Bonny, for helping me realize that I do make a difference.

Thank you to Grandmother Helga, for showing me that there is a difference between getting older and *growing* old. The wisdom and the warmth you show in the winter of your years is an inspiration.

Thank you to Jason and Molly for being patient with your new stepfather.

Thank you to my daughter Kassandra Sunshine for helping me experience God's miracle of creation.

Thank you to all the many other wonderful personal and professional friends who, I am happy to say, are too numerous to mention. You have supported, encouraged, taught, mentored, cared for, and believed in me. You know who you are. Thank you!

Thank you to Columbia Pacific University in San Rafael, California, for operating on the premise that what the student knows is more important than when, where, and how she or he learned it.

Thank you to Shelly Barsuhn for your expertise in developing my manuscript to a point that a publisher would read it and most importantly agree to publish it.

Thank you to Valeria Cindric for your patience, your warmth, your professionalism, and your belief in my work and this book.

Thank you to David L. Young for your valuable editing expertise, your commitment to this book, and your friendship.

Most of all, thank you to Almighty God for creating me and for sending Jesus Christ, who died for me, Whose Spirit guides me and Who will return to take me home.

Foreword

Today's fast-moving, competitive society demands that each of us actively seek integrated care of our body, mind, and spirit. In my many years as a clinician, teacher, and researcher, I have learned that certain actions make us well, or help us recover, and other actions make us sick, or delay our recovery.

Physical health is aided by selected positive behaviors—like vigorous exercise, good nutrition, effective stress management—and harmed by negative behaviors—like sedentary lifestyles, smoking, alcohol abuse.

Mental health is enhanced by certain practices—like good parenting, learning opportunities, pleasant relationships—and stymied by adverse ones—like conflict, violence, prejudice.

Spiritual health is improved by positive attitudes—religious faith, loving and caring relationships, forgiveness—and decreased by others—lack of faith, dishonest relationships, lack of forgiveness.

Whole person health needs physical, mental, and spiritual nurturing. It requires balance. Ron has captured the importance of this balance and provides prescriptions for persons who want to have a happy and productive life. He offers guidance on: how to be at peace with who you are; where you are in life; and where you are going.

Keith W. Sehnert, M.D.
Minneapolis, Minnesota
Author of *Stress/Unstress, Selfcare/Wellcare,*
and *Balancing Act: Body/Mind/Spirit*

Contents

Preface

I've often been asked how and why I got interested in the work I do. For several years I didn't have a good answer. Then, a little over a year ago, in a conversation with my wife, I began to recall that as a youngster I needed a lot of tender loving care to keep me functioning. In fact, I had to be watched very closely so I didn't destroy myself. I had more than my share of bumps, cuts, scrapes, bruises, and broken bones, not to mention all the typical childhood illnesses.

I'm sure my interest in learning how to take care of myself began as a result of experiencing so much pain and discomfort as a child. I remember the doctor saying to my mother, "If I had one more patient as active as Ron, I'd make a great living with just two patients."

Somewhere along the line I concluded that being sick or hurt was something I wanted to avoid. I also concluded that in spite of the cost of living, I preferred it over the alternative! Yes, my health history was probably a *major* factor in my becoming a student of and ultimately a speaker and author on the subject of lifestyle management.

But, I discovered early in my research that a healthy lifestyle is more than just physical. A healthy lifestyle encompasses the mind, body, and spirit. The further I explored wellness, the more convinced I became that it is impossible to be totally healthy physically without being mentally and spiritually healthy as well. The more I learned, the more I began to realize the tremendous synergistic power available to us when the mind, body, and spirit are healthy and in harmony.

A Healthy Body, Mind, and Spirit

Some people spend most of their lives focusing on the development of one, or at most two, of these areas. For example, the intellectual will constantly seek ways to expand his or her mind as if understanding or knowing everything will reveal their reason for being.

The materialist becomes obsessed with the body and the world around them as if what they have and how they look is their reason for being. The spiritualist strives so diligently to live in the spirit that he or she neglects the mind and body—as if life on earth is something to "get through" until moving into the hereafter.

It is important for us to recognize the value of cultivating and growing in *each* of these areas. A consistent growth and balance will allow us to function most optimally.

It is sad to think how many people may miss the opportunity and the excitement of functioning at this level. Because they haven't taken care of themselves, they experience mental, physical, and spiritual bankruptcy instead.

There is a Better Way

Learning to manage your lifestyle is as simple as making choices that will make a positive difference. To the extent that you responsibly *avoid what hinders you* and *make responsible use of what helps you,* you'll achieve what you desire most.

This book is written for people who truly desire to create a lifestyle that will make a positive difference in themselves and others. If this is your desire, congratulations—this book is for you!

Part One

How's Your Lifestyle?

1

Are You Getting the Most Out of Life?

Most of us are concerned about our health. According to a survey by *Industry Week*, 73 percent of the executives polled confided that their biggest overall worry centered around their own well-being—their health. Additionally, 49 percent of them worried about the lack of time for family and leisure activities.

This is in line with a five-year study of executives from fourteen major corporations directed by Dr. Kenneth Pelletier of the USC-San Francisco Medical School. The study revealed that only 7 percent of "successful" people truly lead the exemplary "good life" that success promises.

The study concluded that 93 percent gave up important aspects of their lives to get to the top. They suffered from ill health and broken personal and family relationships, which made it difficult, if not impossible, to enjoy their "success."

What robs people of the joy of living and keeps them from getting the most out of life? Maybe the following illustration will help us draw some conclusions.

No Trade-Ins

When you buy a new car, it practically exudes vitality. The parts all function, the body is rust-free, and the paint is slick and shiny. You don't need to do a thing to make it run efficiently—just hop in.

For the first year or two, it's always ready to go. It starts on the first try, and it can be pushed to top speeds. Besides needing an occasional minor adjustment, your new automobile runs like a dream.

Then, one day, reality strikes. The car begins to rust; you notice the first signs creeping up around the fender. Some cold mornings the engine barely starts. Results cannot be expected without maintenance. No longer can you rev it up and push it to the limit without feeling its age. Your car has become the victim of normal wear and tear.

Most of us avoid this whole depressing scenario by trading in our cars every few years. But we can't do that with our bodies. Some of the parts can be replaced, but, basically, we get one body at birth and it's ours for life.

During our carefree, youthful years, we think our bodies are going to last forever. They've performed well in the past so what could possibly go wrong? We pay little attention to our physical condition, forgetting that as bodies get older they need special maintenance.

As we travel more and more miles, natural deterioration is inevitable. The accumulated wear and tear is normal, but it can be managed and controlled. To counteract this natural deterioration, we must learn to take care of our bodies just as well or better than we do our cars.

Life at the Top

People who juggle career, family, and personal ambition feel in fine shape at the foot of the mountain. But what happens when the stress of the race becomes intense? What happens if the strain is sustained over a long period of time?

The last thing high achievers want once they're two-thirds up the mountain of life is to blow a piston. At 5,000 feet, the strain of the high, thin air starts, and our bodies must be prepared ahead of time. There's a substantial difference between a Sunday family drive and the Pike's Peak Rally.

Before each race, the high performance person gets out the preventive maintenance checklist. They add a higher grade of oil and fuel to their machines. They check the engine, the carburetor, the shocks, the steering, tires, and the brakes. The high performance person gets a firsthand feel for the very pulse of his vehicle. They prepare, adapt, and adjust for higher speeds and a thinner atmosphere to insure peak performance.

Even though it's a hard race, top performers *choose* to live in the uncommon, upper atmosphere. The demands are great, but so are the rewards. Not everyone can handle it. But the high-achieving person can. Why? Because he or she comes to the race prepared with the lasting, peak-performance energy that is available to them on demand.

Yes, your ability to manage the difficult problems, challenges, and changes of daily living is decided by how well you *prepare.* Whenever an opportunity or a crisis places a demand on you, your predetermined energy level will be put to the test.

When you are prepared, when you bring a full reservoir of energy to the challenges and opportunities that come your way, chances are excellent that you will be able to adapt and respond positively. Remember, in a race the first requirement for winning is being able to finish.

Results that Make a Difference

Regardless of what level of health, love, and success you are currently experiencing, imagine for a moment how much better it could be. The ideas and exercises in this book have been carefully researched and selected to produce *results that make a difference.* Their power is in their simplicity.

In order to experience the full benefit of these guidelines, you need to commit time and perseverance to their practice. If you're groaning at the thought, think of the car analogy again. Race car drivers consider the maintenance of their cars as a crucially important time out from the race. They look forward to this "down" time because it helps them achieve results. Preparation time is quality time.

You and I can bring this same attitude to the maintenance of our own bodies. We can integrate these qualities into our daily lives and insure that we are prepared for our consistently fast-paced, ever-changing lifestyles.

Major Hazards to Your Health

Throughout this book, you will be reviewing methods of managing the mind, the body, and the environment. You will learn why the primary cause of disease is neither bacteria nor viruses but weakened resistance brought about by our own health-destroying lifestyles.

In the past, human mortality was largely due to circumstances beyond control. Throughout the centuries, human beings have been vulnerable to contagious diseases such as typhoid fever, polio, and tuberculosis. That is why two thousand years ago, life expectancy was only twenty-two years. By 1884, it had risen, but it was still only forty-four years. Today, our life expectancy is seventy-three plus years, mainly because of improvements in environmental sanitation and medicine.

In the past, the first twenty years of life were critical, and many people did not survive. In the twentieth century, our chances of survival are excellent—except when we sabotage ourselves. The major health hazards we face and the ways we most often die are *not* related to contagious disease or to causes beyond our control. *Public health enemy number one is the way we live—our lifestyles.*

The Center for Disease Control in Atlanta tells us that the major contributing factor in eight out of ten of our society's leading causes of death is *lifestyle.* The big four major health hazards today are heart disease, cancer, motor vehicle accidents, and diabetes. Throughout this book we will investigate the attitudes and habits that contribute to these hazards. More importantly, though, we will also be investigating the attitudes and habits that contribute to the "good life."

The Many Facets of Success

You and I have been given a stereotype of success—what it feels like and what it has to cost our health and peace of mind. Most of us perceive the successful person as one who rushes from meeting to meeting, downing coffee and Maalox as though, without exception, achievement goes hand in hand with ulcers, bad nerves, and a multitude of other ailments.

This stereotype of success, however, doesn't have to become reality. After more than twelve years of study and research, I have found that a highly productive, "successful" life can be yours without the loss of your capacity to enjoy it. It just takes a little more planning than most people are willing to do.

Success has many facets. It can be represented in such achievements as peace of mind, meaningful relationships, purposeful work, financial security, and good health. All these attainments can be yours and at the same time allow you to function effectively in the midst of our hectic, modern day world.

When you, like thousands of others, begin to do your best to realize God's full potential for you and help others do the same, you will be what I call a "living-to-win person."

What is Living to Win?

Living to win is an attitude that fosters total health of mind, body, and spirit.

Living to win is a journey, not a destination. This journey is made by people who, through their commitment to this ideal, experience both a good living and a good life.

People who live to win may be striving to be "number one," but they are seeking a life that has enjoyment, fulfillment, and purpose. They want to make a difference, and *doing* their best is more important than *being* the best.

Their deepest desire goes beyond enjoyment to a supreme purpose that gives wholeness and direction to their lives. They realize, as I did a dozen or so years ago, that they will never experience true joy without the belief that their lives are significant and meaningful.

The Will to Overcome

My friend Earl Oliver exemplifies a "living-to-win person."

In 1952 Earl was happily married, had a steady job as a mail carrier, and was the proud father of a young son. Then he developed an illness that threatened his life. The diagnosis was polio.

For six months Earl was confined to an iron lung. Literally fighting for his life, this healthy 145-pound man shrunk to 70 pounds. When he was finally well enough to leave the confines of the artificial lung, he was paralyzed from the neck down and had to be fed through a tube in his nose.

During the following six months, Earl realized that he would never deliver mail again. Furthermore, he discovered that he had not been employed long enough to be eligible to collect a disability pension; he was one month short. How, he wondered, would he support his family?

Through therapy, Earl gained enough use of his hands and arms to learn a skill; a relative trained him to retouch photographic negatives. Earl began earning money again—not enough, of course, to make up for his previous salary—but it was progress.

It had been a year since the beginning of his bout with polio, and Earl Oliver came home.

At this point, Earl's wife left him. Earl, who was barely able to care for himself, suddenly had sole responsibility for the care of their seven-year-old son.

Then, in the summer of 1954, Earl met Dorothy, the widowed mother of a young daughter. Six months later Earl and Dorothy were married. Two more sons and a daughter were born. Earl and his wife worked hard—and successfully—at providing a home for their five children.

Today the kids are on their own, and Earl is now retired from a successful bookstore and health food business. Although relatively confined to a wheel chair, he exercises on a stationary bicycle, a rowing machine, and a mini trampoline daily. Earl Oliver is one of the healthiest persons I have ever met.

Listen to what Earl Oliver says about himself:

> I've never felt handicapped. There have always been things I couldn't do—before I had polio and after. It's more important what I can do. Everyone can bring joy into the world—some by walking into a room and some by walking out. I prefer to think of myself as one who brings joy by walking in.

Earl Oliver's story is truly amazing because he had the stamina and the resources to transform himself from a helpless man in an iron lung to a successful parent and business achiever. He maintained the desire to do his best and to help others do the same. Earl created a lifestyle he could live with.

Are You Throwing Your Life Away?

Most people would agree that the thought of throwing away a whole life all at once seems foolish, yet countless men and women give little thought to throwing it away in bits and pieces. It is a sad fact that most people spend the first two-thirds of their lives making money and losing their health and the final third spending money in an effort to regain their health.

Throughout the chapters ahead, my goal will be to help you create a healthy lifestyle management system. Once you learn how to maximize your personal resources, you'll begin to realize just how much of a difference you can make, whether it be as a parent, executive, employee, or friend.

Regardless of your age, you can make a difference. Some people say they feel better at fifty, sixty, or seventy than they did at twenty-five. In jest, a client of mine said, "Anybody who can still do at sixty what he was doing at twenty probably wasn't doing much at twenty."

Making the Right Choices

People who enjoy themselves and continue to grow, regardless of their age, make choices of moderation that bring balance, energy, and a sense of purpose into their lives. They avoid the things that hinder them and make responsible use of the things that help them.

My good friend Marilyn Corrigan, a training manager, has been practicing a healthy stress and lifestyle management system for a number of years. She has this to say about its effect on her life:

> Since I began to take the stress and lifestyle management techniques seriously, I have been "in process"—on a continuum, working my way slowly from a very poor stress and lifestyle manager to an above average manager. As a result I have more energy, I'm healthier, and I'm more productive.
>
> This path has not always been smooth. The end result, however, is that I have increased the ways I take care of myself. The rewards have been well

worth it. In the past several years, I have learned
from numerous personal and professional
experiences that it is easy to reach a burn-out state
and very hard to reverse it. Only as I've learned
to make the right choices and to take better care
of myself, I'm enjoying a healthier and a more
enriched life with increased quality and meaning.

A Few Moments a Day

By applying the principles in this book, you'll also
significantly enhance the likelihood of feeling good, living
longer, and doing the things you want to do—just as Earl
Oliver has—without self-imposed restrictions. You will most
certainly improve your ability to realize your fullest God-
given potential, which is likely greater than you can
currently imagine.

A few moments a day can help you know what it's like
to be both dynamically calm and highly productive. A few
moments a day will help you see how much more you can
accomplish when you are at ease or when you are ready to
perform at your optimum.

A few moments a day will help you experience how much
more useful you can be to others when you've taken care
of yourself. Whatever your goals—whatever your purpose
in life—by making the right choices you can attain them.

By studying healthy, high-performance people like Earl
plus hundreds of others, I have discovered certain qualities
that are applicable and transferable to virtually *anyone*. You
can create a lifestyle that will help you enjoy the "good
life"—a lifestyle you can *live* with.

2

How Stress Affects Your Health

One particular characteristic appears consistently in the most successful people I have studied. In fact, it is one of the most important traits they possess—*the ability to deal with stress.*

Osborn Segerberg, author of the book, *Living To 100—1200 Who Did and How They Did It,* discovered that the common thread to longevity among a varied group of centenarians was the effective way in which they handled stress.

Fortified by the will to live, as well as an apparently innate knowledge of how to care for themselves, these centenarians were prepared when the inevitable stresses of life came their way. Their ability to manage and make responsible use of stress made the difference.

Poorly Managed Stress

Stress has been called the disease of the twentieth century. It is the wild beast facing modern men and women, and it is everywhere.

—The student bites his fingernails, waiting for the instructor to pass out the exam.

—The inexperienced speaker feels lightheaded and cotton-mouthed standing in front of an audience.

—The mother breaks into a sweat when her young son's temperature suddenly rises to 104 degrees.

—The broker experiences a gnawing stomach pain while watching the market plunge.

—The realtor's shoulders tighten painfully when he hears that the deal fell through.

—The husband's head begins to pound as he pays the monthly bills and balances the checkbook.

When managed poorly, the stress created during these situations and countless others can change our personalities, modify our perceptions, cloud our feelings and attitudes, and adversely affect our behavior and health.

Notice I said "managed poorly." Stress alone does not produce the ill effects we will be discussing; the poor management of stress, however, does.

Stress Can Make You Sick

Stress has been proven to be a contributing factor in:

- Common colds
- Headaches
- Fatigue
- Stomach aches
- Hay fever
- Skin rashes
- Asthma
- Muscle tension

It has even been accountable for contributing to such serious diseases as:

- Cancer
- Heart disease
- Colitis
- Epilepsy
- Rheumatoid arthritis

In fact, stress can be linked to just about any malady you can think of. My conservative estimate is that poorly handled stress contributes to at least 80 percent of all accidents and illnesses.

American businesses lose an estimated $100 billion annually because of premature death and health-related absenteeism due to poorly-managed stress. Dr. Richard O. Keeler of the President's Council on Physical Fitness and Sports observes,

> It is a tragedy of the [business] professions that so many sales people, managers, and executives are struck down at the peak of their productive years by degenerative diseases related to stress and sedentary lifestyles.

Poorly-managed stress is still by far the number one robber of creativity, health, and productivity.

The Effects of Stress

Now let's look at some of the effects of stress. Among them are:

- Hair twisting
- Nail biting
- Nervous ticks

- Fist clenching
- Jaw tightening

As stress progresses, more serious reactions can occur, such as:

- Overeating
- Overdrinking
- Depression
- Drug dependence
- Smoking
- Violence
- Suicide

Recently there has been so much media attention paid to stress that the publicity may actually be *causing* stress! Why? Because most people still do not understand stress or know how to manage it.

Stress in and of itself is not negative. Stress is an inevitable by-product of life, especially of achievement-oriented lifestyles. It is *not* an invisible monster lurking like some infectious disease, ready at any moment to spring up unexpectedly.

Although stress *is* inevitable, its ill-effects are not.

Stress Management is Energy Management

Stress is your body's reaction to any demand placed upon it. This simple definition makes no judgment about stress being bad, or good, or both. It simply states what stress is—a reaction to a demand.

We place a demand on our bodies when we get out of bed in the morning, walk the dog, drive to work, meet with our boss, or greet someone special. Everyone experiences demands—stress. The only people who don't experience stress are dead! Even normal bodily functions are responses to demands. Our bodies' functions are forms of stress that sustain life.

Over the years, I've used the following method to help people understand what stress is: Each time you see the word *stress,* replace it with the word *energy.* For example, if you manage your stress well, you manage your energy well. Conversely, if you manage your energy well, you manage your stress well.

Little demands placed upon your body cause a little stress and require little energy. Big demands placed upon your body cause a big stress reaction, which requires a lot of energy. Remember, for all practical purposes, stress management is energy management.

How We React to Stressful Situations

Stress's common denominator is *change.* As long as we live, we will experience thousands of changes every day. Experts say that today we face more changes—more sensory input—in one day than our grandparents faced during their entire lifetimes. Our reactions to stressful situations may be subtle—so subtle we don't even realize they are occurring.

For instance, sometimes we react to seemingly unimportant changes with tension that places a relatively light demand on the body. Problems are created when this sort of tension is permitted to accumulate into a condition referred to as *hypertonus:* too much tension in the muscles. This malady is something like the situation created when the brake and the accelerator of a car are pressed at the same time.

Certain factors, like those listed below, may cause or aggravate stress:

- Too much change
- Poor coping skills

- Lack of exercise
- Inadequate relaxation
- Poor nutrition
- Excessive body weight
- Excessive alcohol intake
- Smoking
- Financial difficulties
- Troubled marriage
- Work
- Personal/family crisis
- Noise
- Poor time management
- Poor support systems at home and at work
- Fast forward (Type "A") attitudes

During any situation involving change, the body can create an enormous amount of pent up energy. As a consequence, a lot of wear and tear (stress) is experienced within. This causes an unnecessary drain on energy reserves.

Other, more obvious, circumstances cause us to react immediately and intensely, producing the fight or flight reaction. This response puts an extremely heavy demand on the body. Perceiving a serious threat, the body is put on red alert in order to make itself respond effectively. The stress producing this fight or flight syndrome is obvious, as the body reacts to a demand placed upon it.

The Fight or Flight Reaction

In order to demonstrate how tension can build slowly and how this accumulation can affect the intensity of the fight or flight reaction, I'd like you to visualize a situation with me.

You are just returning from a pleasant and relaxing vacation. Having settled into your seat on the plane, you lean back to enjoy the memories of the recent days.

Suddenly, the captain's voice over the intercom interrupts your dreamy thoughts: "We will be passing through the outer edges of a storm. There are reports of mild turbulence. To be on the safe side, please fasten your seat belts."

The "Fasten Seat Belt" sign blinks on above your head, and a few minutes pass with the airplane bouncing you slightly.

Then you hear the intercom click on again.

"The turbulence appears to be a little stronger than we originally anticipated," says the captain, "so I'll ask that you remain in your seats, keeping seat belts fastened, until further advised."

During the next few silent moments, the ride becomes quite choppy. Again, the intercom interrupts.

"This is your captain speaking. Place your trays and seats in a forward position. We are approaching the most turbulent area—*oh, my God!*"

The plane lurches forward, you're thrown against the restraints of the seat belt, and people around you scream out. Suddenly, the entire cabin is quiet.

In a few minutes that seem like hours, the captain returns to the intercom. "Ladies and gentlemen, we are now past the worst of the turbulence. And let me apologize for that sudden outburst—I spilled a cup of hot coffee on my lap."

When Stress is Destructive

This brings us to two points. The first is that unlike the subtle reactions to typical daily challenges, the fight or flight reaction is obvious. It definitely gets your attention. When it occurs, you can feel it.

Second, the intensity of your reaction to the captain's outburst is determined by how serious you perceived the threat to be and by how much tension you had accumulated inside. This residual or left over tension is the hypertonus mentioned earlier.

If, in a situation like this, you jumped very little, the residual tension you had stored was probably slight. If you were very startled, your body had probably stored a great deal more residual tension. In other words, it had wound itself a little tighter.

Of course, the threatening situation doesn't have to be life-threatening. It may come in the form of an unexpected noise or occurrence, such as a door slamming. We can't stop these unexpected situations from startling us. But as long as we can get away from the causes periodically in order to stop the reactions, or if we have some way of diffusing or releasing the energy from within, the body will balance itself, regenerate, and replenish energy. I call this the *productive stress cycle.*

When we do not get away from the causes of tension, or when we don't find a way of diffusing and/or releasing this energy, long term bodily imbalances occur internally. These imbalances are highly destructive, sapping energy reserves and resulting in exhaustion and dysfunction. This I call the *destructive stress cycle.*

No wonder headaches, backaches, and stomachaches are commonplace at the end of a typical day.

The Grizzly Bear Syndrome

Imagine another stressful situation. It will, I hope, show how important it is to avoid the cause of internal imbalance and to release accumulated tensions inside the body.

You've gone camping with your family and have just spent the day backpacking into the mountains. It was a rigorous but fascinating journey. The wild flowers were in bloom, and you even walked behind a sparkling waterfall.

Now it's evening, and the fire has died into a few glowing embers. Everyone's asleep, but you're not quite finished relishing the peacefulness of this beautiful day.

You decide to take a short walk under a clear, star-bright sky. Walking up the trail a bit, you smell pine and feel an evening breeze against your face. You're relaxed and more content than you've been in years.

Then, suddenly, ahead of you to the right, you spot a dark figure in a grove of trees.

It's a grizzly bear!

Immediately an involuntary metabolic change occurs. A threat to your survival is perceived, and your body is instantly alarmed and alert. Without your even realizing it, your heart-rate, blood pressure, rate of breathing, blood flow, muscle tension, blood clotting agents, white blood cell count, and body metabolism increase dramatically.

Within six to eight seconds, your entire body is activated for one of the oldest, innate reactions of which the human body is capable—fight or flight. Your body naturally adapts to this new set of circumstances.

Without your conscious participation, your endocrine system releases thousands of full-strength hormones into the bloodstream, and your autonomic nervous system sends impulses filled with thousands of instructions to all parts of your body—and at tremendous speeds of 200-300 miles per hour.

Being of sound mind, you decide to run.

It doesn't matter one bit whether there actually is a grizzly bear in those bushes or whether you just imagined one. Somewhere you've learned that bears can be hazardous to your health, and that knowledge, along with the perceived threat to your survival, is enough to set off a whole chain of physical reactions.

Of course, the run back to camp releases some accumulated tension; that's positive. But even after you get back to camp and relative safety, the tension isn't over. You can't get that grizzly bear out of your mind. You lie awake listening to every noise—the wind now sounds eerie as it whistles through the trees, and every crack of a branch is the grizzly bear coming to get you. Even as you're snuggled safely into your warm sleeping bag, your vivid imagination races, remembering every gruesome bear story you've ever heard.

Worry—the Energy Thief

The familiar terminology for this type of imagination is *worry,* and as long as you keep worrying and replaying the incident in your mind, the alarm continues. Your body remains alert. Stress is prolonged as long as you harbor the thought of danger. Your body, including the brain cells, is unable to regenerate and regain its balance. Your system remains in a state of attention.

In this condition, you drain your own energy reserves, keep muscle tension mercilessly taut, and involve your brain, heart, and liver in a complex chemical process that can push them to their highest capacity without relief.

This distress, whether from a real or imagined source, does two things: it sustains tensions and intense bodily changes, and it drains energy needlessly. These are tremendous demands on your body's metabolism. When they are allowed to persist, imbalances like this sabotage your health.

Maintaining Your Balance

Internal balance is the single most important ingredient to creating a lifestyle you can live with. If you and I want to experience optimal health in our lives, we must find responsible ways to avoid the causes of unnecessary stress; and we must find ways to release or diffuse tensions. Consistently, we must find ways to return to balance, which will enable us to conserve, regenerate, and replenish energy.

I'm not saying that we must maintain balance 100 percent of the time. That's impossible. In fact, it's undesirable. Without stress and the resultant imbalance, there would be no spice of life. There would be no laughter and no tears. There would be no opportunity to progress and grow through experience.

Imbalance—for a time—can be productive. But when pressures exceed the level at which we can handle them and still perform effectively, imbalance stops being productive. At this point, the demands placed on the body deplete energy reserves to near exhaustion. The body becomes increasingly vulnerable to health hazards.

When You're Pushed to the Limit

Nothing is wrong with hard work and hard play. Occasionally it feels good to push ourselves to the limit, as long as we give our bodies the chance to regenerate and balance themselves.

When you and I lose the ability to "unhook"—let go—we're no longer in control. The body's natural self-regulation system, which controls our temperature, the oxygenation of the blood, our level of sodium and potassium, and countless other functions, becomes confused. Imbalance allowed to go on and on gradually shifts the body's *homeostatic* (i.e., natural) balances.

The body adjusts itself to new, less healthy levels of blood pressure, heart-rate, or overall body metabolism. The longer this state goes unchecked, the greater the chance of harm. Because poorly managed stress takes its toll on your immune system, it lowers your body's natural defense against anything from the common cold to a dreadful disease such as AIDS. The result is almost inevitable: chronic disease.

Excessive stress may cause or aggravate:

- Atherosclerosis
- High blood pressure
- Vascular disease
- Heart failure
- Stroke
- Alcohol abuse and alcoholism
- A motor vehicle accident
- Diabetes
- Cancer

- Suicide
- Homicide
- Premature death

This is why it is vital to *avoid* constant internal imbalances that drain us and to make responsible use of regular internal balance, which regenerates us. The good news is that we are capable of learning how to bring our bodies back into balance and maintain high energy levels.

What Makes Stress Dangerous?

Dramatic experiences with airplanes and grizzly bears are, in many ways, easier to deal with than the more subtle, everyday tension-creating experiences. When something out of the ordinary gives us a scare, we *know* we've been pushed out of balance. Common irritants, on the other hand, may be initially less jarring, but the human body has a tendency to bottle these tensions.

Further complicating the condition is our tendency to become de-sensitized. And this is *the most dangerous aspect of the stress syndrome.* The majority of affected people don't even realize they're victims.

It is said that if you drop a frog into a pot of boiling water, it will immediately hop out—and survive. If, however, that same frog is placed in room temperature water that is leisurely brought to a boil, the frog, without protest, will slowly be overcome by the heat.

Dr. Rene Dubos identified the problem succinctly: "What I fear is our ability to adjust." Notice—that was our *ability* to adjust, not *inability*.

People adapt so readily to the tensions they experience every day—noise, traffic jams, work, family situations—that they don't even feel the enormous irritation and energy drain they're experiencing. Feeling tense, having aches and pains, and feeling rushed and pressured begin to seem normal.

How Noise Affects Your Stress Level

Three hundred years ago, actual noise as we know it was confined to natural events over which humans had no control. America sounded like wilderness—wolves howled, trees toppled, and water rushed over waterfalls and ran down mountain streams.

Today, surrounded by sounds difficult to escape—jetliners, motorcycles, snowmobiles, lawn mowers, chain saws, tractors, traffic, sirens, jack hammers—we step inside our homes to be bombarded further by televisions, radios, electric razors, hair blowers, and air conditioners. At the office, it may mean another eight-plus hours of uninterrupted din. In our society, we move from one deafening environment to another.

We're so accustomed to the clamor that we don't even hear it, not really. People exposed to the same noises each day, especially loud ones, adapt so well that after an adjustment period, they don't consciously "hear" it anymore.

Unfortunately, our "desensitizing" of noises doesn't make them any less harmful. Even when we're not aware of them, sounds—especially sudden ones—evoke a rapid, increased blood flow, raising the heart-rate and, ultimately, elevating blood pressure. This is the body's method of responding to stress in what is called a *stress reaction*.

Researchers Dr. Ernest A. Peterson and Dr. Jeffrey S. Augenstein of the University of Miami School of Medicine experimented with the effects of noise. Two rhesus monkeys were selected for the test because their hearts and circulatory systems were "the closest [they] could get to humans." The doctors subjected the monkeys to the same kinds of noises heard daily by the typical blue collar worker in America. At the end of three weeks, the animals' blood pressure had jumped 43 percent.

What is a safe noise level? Although researchers aren't yet sure, it is obvious that what many of us consider "normal" is not safe. Even people who believe they're handling stress and the everyday pressures of life well aren't as tension-free as they think they are.

Can you remember the "good old days" when the still, small voice within us used to be called "conscience" instead of "transistor radio"? Pursuing the sounds of silence will enhance your health.

Action Alternatives

You may be surprised to discover that more than 50 percent of the factors that cause heart disease and stroke are related to lifestyle—the way we eat, drink, think, and take care of ourselves.

If you have come to the conclusion that stress is affecting your health and your life, there is something you can do about it. To help lower your risk of having the stress related dysfunctions mentioned earlier, try putting some of these suggestions into practice:

- Develop optimistic attitudes
- Improve your support systems
- Exercise regularly and vigorously
- Learn to manage change
- Improve your time management skills
- Improve rest habits
- Improve nutritional intake
- Reduce body weight
- Reduce alcohol intake
- Stop smoking
- Get a complete physical exam

Because these lifestyle alternatives will help you enjoy the quality of life you desire, we will be discussing them in greater detail in the chapters ahead.

3
Managing Fast-Forward Behavior

Before you can learn to handle pressure, it's necessary to understand yourself. A good way to begin this process is to make an honest appraisal of your personality style. Ask yourself these questions:

1. Do I often perform more than one task simultaneously (eat and work, dress and read, etc.)?
2. Do I often get restless when I have to wait in line?
3. After a hard day's work, do I often have difficulty relaxing?
4. Have others who know me well advised me to slow down?
5. Am I a fast driver? a fast eater?
6. Do I bring work home more than once a week?
7. Do I often keep my emotions (anger) inside?

If you answered "yes" to a majority of these questions, chances are your personality leans more toward the "fast-forward" mode. People with these characteristics have typically been called *Type "A" personalities.*

I prefer the term *fast-forward* because, like a recorder, Type "A" people do operate in other modes—slow motion, pause, and reverse. Generally, however, they tend to get stuck in fast-forward. And this is where they get into trouble.

Certain lifestyle factors contribute to or aggravate Type "A" attitudes in people. In addition, the way a fast-forward person lives also adds to the stress and strain he or she is already experiencing. Some of these factors are:

- Time pressures
- Poor ability to delegate
- Stress or change
- Can't say no
- Faulty nutrition
- Excessive intake of sugar and caffeine
- Lack of exercise
- Smoking

Are You Stuck in Fast-Forward?

As I stated earlier, being out of balance is not in itself destructive; but to the extent an individual cannot let go and return to a healthy balance, she or he is no longer in control.

People with fast-forward personalities eat, walk, and talk fast. They are restless and impatient, have trouble relaxing, and thrive on deadlines. Typically they are compulsive, competitive, and power-seeking. They are clock-watchers and time-binders. Fast-forward types will try to cram eight hours of work into two and then become agitated when the work isn't completed—especially if someone else was expected to do it.

They feel pressure even when there's no need to. They burn a great deal of energy needlessly and have trouble unhooking. They are the high rollers—big spenders—when it comes to energy use.

About 2 a.m. in an airport rest room, I was at the sink washing my hands. At first I thought I was alone in the room, but I kept hearing a faint mumbling. Turning to look, I saw a pair of legs at the end of a long row of stalls. Listening more closely, I quickly realized that the gentleman in the stall was dictating a letter to his secretary!

Some people might call that an efficient use of time. I say it demonstrates a number of points about fast-forward personalities: the need to do more than one thing at a time, a tendency to have trouble letting go, and an inclination to be stuck in the fast-forward mode.

Ten Tips to an Early Grave

For those of you with dominant fast-forward personalities, let me save you a little time by giving you *Ten Tips to an Early Grave:*

1. Make sure your job comes first and your personal and family life second.

2. Go to work evenings, weekends, and holidays so you won't be interrupted.

3. When not at work, spend time at home thinking about or doing work to catch up or get ahead.

4. Drive fast because you can't waste time getting where you need to be.

5. Consistently plan meetings for breakfast, lunch, or dinner.

6. Avoid time wasters like hunting, fishing, golf, gardening, and regular exercise.

7. Be involved in as many organizations, committees, meetings, and banquets as possible.

8. Take vacations only when absolutely necessary.

9. When out of town for work, schedule an early morning appointment for your first day back at your office to help keep you on track.

10. Do not delegate responsibility; you can do it better and faster yourself.

One thing is for sure: You'll never get too busy to attend your own funeral, whether or not it was in your schedule.

Are There Advantages to Being a Slow-Motion Person?

If your answers to the seven personality evaluation questions were primarily "no's," you are most likely a *Type "B."* Most often in the slow-motion mode, Type "B" personalities are definitely unhooked.

They read slowly, eat slowly, speak slowly—and generally drive fast-forward people crazy! Slow-motion people are easy-going and rarely harried. They take time. They're contemplative, steady-working, and not easily irritated.

I'm not saying that one type of personality is better than the other. The stuck, fast-forward people, without management, can drive themselves into an early grave. On the other hand, the stuck slow-motion people, without a little motivation, can bore themselves to death. Knowing which personality style describes you is not as important as knowing your own tendencies and learning how to manage them.

People who meet me for the first time rarely think I'm a fast-forward person, but a closer evaluation of my behavior clearly shows that I am. After training, however, I've learned to manage myself relatively well.

This training has been well worth my time because my research shows that fast-forward people make up only 20 percent of the population, yet they account for 80 percent of the people who have heart disease.

Coronary heart disease is common in fast-forward people in their thirties or forties, while slow-motion people rarely experience heart trouble before age seventy. The life span of the average fast-forward individual is fourteen years shorter than her or his slow-motion counterpart—fifty-nine years compared to seventy-three.

Who Accomplishes More?

In one of my seminars, a participant who clearly exhibited fast-forward characteristics responded to this data by saying, "That makes sense, because it will only take me fifty-nine years to accomplish what it takes those slow-motion folks seventy-three years to do." He said it in jest, but, let me assure you, it is not true.

Furthermore, a lot can be experienced and accomplished during those additional fourteen years. More than one survey has shown that a majority of the very top executives who are highly efficient and productive have more slow-motion characteristics than fast-forward. These people work out of a sense of purpose rather than compulsion. They enjoy their play time and set aside time for their loved ones. Most important, they know their worth apart from their work. They know they are worthy individuals because of who they are.

What is a Workaholic?

Workaholics, who are most likely fast-forward people, may succeed—but often *in spite of* their destructive habits, not because of them. Let's look at some characteristics of a workaholic.

These men and women work intensely to escape failure. They feel compelled to win in order to feel worthwhile. They have great difficulty determining the difference between having a failure and being one. They rarely ever slow down let alone stop, and, consequently, they rarely replenish their energy supply. They don't actually come home from the office; they come home *with* it. Friday means two more working days until Monday.

Workaholics pay a high price for compulsive behavior. Generally, they make a good living, but—all too often—without making much of a life. They take extraordinary risks with their health and their families.

> Susie, a third-grader, pulled up her chair to the dinner table.
>
> "Where's Daddy?" she asked, plaintively.
>
> Her mother explained gently to her, "Daddy had some work to finish up at the office."
>
> The next evening, the same scenario was repeated.
>
> Susie asked, "Where's Daddy?"
>
> "Daddy had some work to finish up at the office," her mother replied.
>
> Susie considered this.
>
> "Mom," she said, "Daddy always has lots of work to catch up on. Can't they put him in a slower group?"

Workaholics like this rarely make the best workers; their tendency is to compete rather than cooperate—to collect too much data and then have trouble focusing and establishing priorities. Most of the time, workaholics and/or fast-forwards are too stressed to be creative and don't—or won't—delegate authority and responsibility because they feel no one can do the job well enough to suit them.

How to Manage Fast-Forward Behavior

Almost all of us have some Type "A" personality tendencies. But we can learn to manage our behavior by changing our lifestyle and using these traits to our advantage. Here are some suggestions you may want to try:

1. Don't rush your life unnecessarily ("hurry sickness"). Slow down your pace of eating, drinking, driving, and working when appropriate.

2. Prioritize the things you need done, do one thing at a time, and delegate what others can do.

3. Give yourself plenty of time for each task or event. Don't schedule appointments too close together.

4. Learn to say no. You can't do everything. This will help reduce your number of deadlines, self-imposed or otherwise.

5. Avoid the hurried sandwich at your desk, and reduce working lunches. Get away, and give yourself a break.

6. Avoid taking your work home. It will be there tomorrow. Finish it then.

7. Keep fresh; don't do things the same way all the time.

8. Become more flexible and less of a perfectionist.

9. Increase listening time and decrease talking time. Fast-forward people have a tendency to verbalize too much.

10. Spend more time cultivating relationships with Type "B" (slow motion) people.

11. Get up thirty minutes early to give yourself more quality time to visit with your family and dress without rushing.

12. Set aside an hour a day to be alone, relax, read, walk, or just reflect.

13. Insist on having a time and place at home where you can be alone without being interrupted.

14. Admit you are wrong, forgive yourself, and move forward.

15. Most important, love and respect yourself.

The most realistic way for you to begin practicing these tips is to choose a minimum of two and a maximum of four that you feel will be helpful for you. Start with those and add others as you see your behavior improve.

Heredity or Lifestyle?

For a rather serious example of the risks some people are willing to take with their health and families, let's look briefly at the lives of Mary Parke and Fred Miller.

Mary is a wife and mother of three. She works a part-time job and is involved in countless volunteer activities. At age forty-seven, she was diagnosed as having cancer in both lungs.

Then there's Fred, who's been climbing the corporate ladder for the past twenty years. Whether at home or at work, Fred travels in the fast lane. Shortly before his forty-third birthday, Fred suffered a near-fatal heart attack.

Heredity, of course, may have played a part in the development of these life-threatening diseases. But did these illnesses otherwise develop by chance? The answer is a resounding *no!*

Actually, our lifestyles and lifelong habits have much more to do with our fates than we realize. I always view the nature of heredity as similar to a game of cards. The hand you are dealt isn't as important, many times, as how you *play* what you are dealt. For instance, few people would consciously choose to be ill. Yet the choices they make—or don't make—do add up to the kind of health they will experience.

Mary's and Fred's personalities and lifestyles indicated that they were both headed for trouble many years before their illnesses actually occurred. Each was a smoker, had put on weight, and had neglected exercise for years. Although both considered themselves healthy until disaster struck, so did the frog before gradually being overcome by slowly heating water!

According to the Center for Disease Control, *you*—not your husband or wife, not the doctor, not your parents or grandparents, but *you*—control more than 50 percent of the factors that cause heart attack and stroke. The way you choose to live determines the condition of your heart.

Heart Attack and Stroke

Approximately 675,000 Americans die from heart attack each year—more than in any other country. Each year about

500,000 Americans have a stroke and around 175,000 die as a result.

Medically speaking, a heart attack is a "myocardial infarction" that happens when one of the coronary arteries in the heart is suddenly and completely blocked. This blockage of blood flow kills that portion of the heart.

A stroke results from damage to the brain cells as a result of a clot in a vessel supplying it blood. Brain damage from a stroke often resists treatment. That's why prevention is so important.

Atherosclerosis—hardening of the arteries—is a slow, progressive disease. Fatty deposits (primarily cholesterol) accumulate and harden on the smooth lining of the coronary arteries that supply blood to the heart. With time, the build-up will protrude into the channel of the vessel and cause blockage. It's similar to the way lime deposits form on the inside of water pipes and prevent the adequate flow of water.

Serious Business

One method of treating advanced atherosclerosis is a heart bypass operation. The chest is completely opened up and doctors attempt to bypass a narrowed coronary artery with another vein (usually one taken from the patient's thigh) or a man-made vessel. This very serious operation is a high price to pay for years of overindulgence in high cholesterol foods and a sedentary lifestyle.

Changing your lifestyle is serious business and not something to be taken lightly. A heart attack or stroke can lead to physical disability, mental disability, and/or premature death. What sets the stage for heart attack and stroke? Several factors may cause or aggravate a potential heart problem.

- Type "A" attitudes
- Workaholism

- Excessive stress (change)
- Lack of exercise
- High blood pressure
- Smoking
- Unhealthy cholesterol levels
- Excessive alcohol intake
- Excessive body weight
- Faulty nutrition
- Diabetes
- Atherosclerosis

A Change of Heart

When Tony began experiencing severe chest pains, he went to his doctor for a check-up. After a series of tests and consultation with a heart specialist, Tony was told he needed to have bypass surgery or risk having a fatal heart attack. Shocked by this unexpected news, Tony requested a second opinion. After another thorough examination, his new physician prescribed heart medication along with a low-fat, low cholesteral diet and moderate exercise.

With diet and exercise information supplied by his doctor, along with his own research into the problem, Tony changed his lifestyle overnight. Over the next three years, each visit to the doctor showed an improvement in cholesterol levels, and medication was reduced each time. Today Tony is healthy and completely off all medication, but he still maintains a low-fat, high-fiber diet and walks nearly everyday.

You can lower your risk of heart and blood vessel disease by changing the way you live and improving your lifestyle in the following ways:

- Reduce Type "A" attitudes
- Workaholism
- Exercise three or more times a week

- Reduce your intake of foods containing fats and cholesterol
- Have blood screened for cholesterol levels at least once a year
- Improve stress management skills
- Monitor your blood pressure
- Improve your nutritional intake
- Reduce excess weight (fat)
- Stop smoking
- Reduce your salt intake
- Reduce caffeine intake
- Reduce alcohol consumption
- Take medication (only when necessary) as prescribed by a heart specialist

Take a Look at Yourself

Successful people who are living to win do not assume that illness can only happen to others. They realize that how they live and how they take care of themselves will affect the quality and vitality of their lives, and they accept the responsibility. These people believe in creating a lifestyle they can live with.

Appraising your tendencies and your attitudes is the first helpful step toward striking a balance in your life. This will help you understand your particular tendencies.

It's important that we accept stress as a reality in our lives and learn to deal with it effectively. How much better to decide on this course of action *before* a crisis. How much better to prevent problems *before* they begin. How much better to responsibly *avoid* what hinders us and to utilize what helps us to achieve what we value most.

Throughout this book, we will consistently develop a lifestyle management system to help you enjoy the "good life" you desire.

4

The Search for Temporary Relief

The Random House Dictionary defines *disease* as "a condition of the body in which there is incorrect function."

There is definitely an incorrect function in the body when we smoke, consume alcohol to excess, lack exercise, eat poorly or destructively, or subject our bodies to excessive distress in a variety of forms.

I'm convinced that the more we understand about the potential hazards of these habits, the more likely we are to select positive health habits and/or commit ourselves to working against destructive patterns.

In this and the next few chapters we will be looking at several destructive lifestyle habits and what we can do to avoid and change them.

Sources of Comfort

You and I face a multitude of demanding situations daily. When we internalize them, consciously or unconsciously, our bodies reflect the stress.

Far too often people will try to mask the effects of a demanding lifestyle. We want to be cool under pressure and in control of ourselves—even if we can't control the circumstances. But when we try to ignore stressful situations, our bodies don't. Our bodies know.

We heighten the problem by resorting to destructive sources of comfort. What are the most common destructive ways Americans deal with the persistent demands of daily life? By eating too much or too little, taking drugs, drinking alcohol, smoking, etc.

A Nation of Hypochondriacs

If someone outside the United States evaluated our health via television commercials, he or she would conclude that virtually every American has either tired blood, indigestion, back aches, headaches, sniffles, sore throats, constipation, or all of the above.

Because of advertising and the accepted uses of over-the-counter drugs in our society, many Americans take pills to relieve everyday pressures.

Norman Cousins, celebrated author of *Anatomy of an Illness,* had this to say about drug consumption: "Americans generally are becoming gutless hypochondriacs, pill poppers, and sissies." As a nation, we consume 20,000 pounds of aspirin yearly. That's 225 tablets for every man, woman, and child. (I'm not taking any, so someone out there is doubling up!)

There's no denying that any drug—from aspirin to narcotics—can provide temporary relief. But they do not treat the source of the problem. Medications often treat the symptom, allowing—in most cases—the real problem to worsen by neglect.

Medications should be viewed as similar to the new inflatable spare tires. They are rarely needed and should be for short term use only. Regardless of your age, reassess your attitude toward the use of *every* drug you take. If you are taking prescribed medications, ask your doctor if they are truly necessary.

No Escape

It's been said that "many drugs are escapes from which there is no escape." Using drugs to manage the demands placed upon us is about as effective as trying to fill a punctured tire with air. It works for awhile, but the tire will soon be flat again. Until you repair the tire, the problems remain. Most likely they'll get worse.

Pain should be viewed as a warning or a symptom of a problem—not as the problem itself, to be eradicated at all costs. Pain medications only block the symptom, allowing the real health threat to worsen by neglect.

In America, drugs like aspirin have become big business. Media images tell us that pain is negative, that we need not experience it, that intelligent people don't tolerate it, you haven't got time for it, and that we must get rid of it immediately. One ad says, "Life got tougher, so we got stronger."

Ads not only promote a product, they tell us that life without pain and discomfort is possible. We are barraged with "scientific" evidence, animated diagrams, and personal testimonials that tout the superiority of one painkiller over another. They tell us we don't have to suffer the consequences of abusing our bodies and that health can be bought.

This is a lie. Never before has there been a society so subjected to such a consumption of poisonous substances. The effects could be catastrophic in the decades ahead.

Everyday Drugs

In the mid 1970s, American drug companies were already producing about five billion doses of amphetamines annually, and doctors busily wrote over two hundred million prescriptions to their patients.

In 1977, the ever-popular tranquilizer, Valium, was prescribed over 100 million times; more than 800 billion tablets were consumed that year. Since then, addictions to minor tranquilizers have boomed. The plain fact is that tranquilizer users run a great risk of becoming dependent on drugs. Ironically, the very drugs that patients use to cope with everyday stress often actually reduce their ability to do so.

Business people under stress commonly use ten times the recommended dosage of tranquilizers. They start out with the normal dose to elicit a cool and controlled facade for important meetings or high-stress business situations. But they end up hooked—*needing* the drugs to maintain the front.

An alarmingly high number of people, especially those in their fifties and sixties, are taking several prescription drugs a day. A *20/20* television program titled "The Elderly—Pills and Problems" investigated the problem. One woman interviewed admitted to taking twenty-two different medications—forty pills a day—during the peak of her drug-taking. Fortunately, her case was brought to the attention of a geriatric psychiatrist who helped her reduce the different medications from twenty-two down to three.

Emerson was right: "The spirit of the world, the great calm presence of the Creator, does not come to the sorceries of opium and wine."

Breaking the Pill Habit

Some of the drugs pushed do more harm than the pain they suppress. Take a look at the *Physician's Desk Reference* in the library. Every drug listed has side effects. Some of them can kill you. Sir William Osler, the first professor of medicine at Johns Hopkins Medical School made this statement: "One of the first duties of the physician is to educate [people] not to take medicine." Obviously, this is contrary to the norm today.

How do we break the pattern? We can reassess our attitudes toward pain. Physicians can help us determine whether the medications we are taking are essential to our health or just making it easier to live with a worsening health threat.

In addition, we can begin to educate ourselves about our own bodies and break our increasing dependence on doctors and drugs. These options represent only a tiny fraction of the healing process. Our bodies are capable of healing themselves much of the time. For more on this topic, read Keith Sehnert's book, *How to Be Your Own Doctor Sometimes* or Robert Mendelson's *Confessions of a Medical Heretic.*

Dangerous and Deadly

In their search for temporary relief, some people go beyond the use of over-the-counter and prescription drugs into the dangerous world of illegal substances.

Marijuana, once thought harmless, has been found to be very dangerous. One of the reasons is that marijuana has changed. It's considerably more potent—about ten times stronger than the pot smoked during the sixties.

Several years ago, the director of the National Institute on Drug Abuse, Dr. Robert L. Dupont, said publicly that marijuana was less a hazard to health than tobacco or alcohol. As a prominent physician, his word was taken seriously and is still being reiterated by proponents of marijuana-smoking.

Since his statement, however, Dr. Dupont has had a complete change of mind. Recent statements include this one:

> We know a lot more about the health hazards of
> marijuana now and how dangerous it really is. I
> get a sick feeling in the pit of my stomach when
> I hear talk about marijuana being safe. Marijuana
> is a very powerful agent which is affecting the
> body in many ways. What the full range of these

consequences is going to prove to be, one can only guess at this point. But from what we already know, I have no doubt they are going to be horrendous.

Not all the health hazards are yet known. But several new facts have been uncovered.

One marijuana cigarette has as much tar as a dozen or more tobacco cigarettes. Smoked in fifteen minutes, it can produce as high a level of carbon monoxide in the bloodstream as ten to twenty cigarettes smoked throughout the day.

According to Nicolas A. Pace, M.D., "It takes ten to twenty years for heavy cigarette smoking to produce the same type of severe sinusitis, pharyngitis, bronchitis, or emphysema than less than a year of daily marijuana smoking produces."

Marijuana contains 50 percent more cancer-causing materials than tobacco. Marijuana is a powerful substance; it does more damage than tobacco and in less time. Since pot reduces the immune system's capacity to resist infection, marijuana-smokers are more prone to illness.

Mistaken Pleasure

Once mistakenly thought of as an aphrodisiac, marijuana decreases sexual desire after a brief initial increase. It causes a *decrease* in the body's production of testosterone, the substance that makes men, men. With regular to heavy use, marijuana will also cause a measurable increase in the number of abnormal sperm cells produced.

Any woman who smokes it while pregnant is also subjecting her unborn child to its effects.

All in all, marijuana contains over 400 known chemicals, sixty of which are known to affect the brain and central nervous systems. They can cause severe anxiety. Marijuana smoking can interfere with memory, intellectual performance, concentration, and reading comprehension, as well as with visual perception and motor skills.

Americans consume an estimated 60 percent of the world's supply of illicit drugs. More money is presently being spent on illegal drugs in America than on food. The figures are so staggering that they become meaningless. Drug abuse is commonplace.

All the data isn't in. Much is left to be researched. But even at this stage, it seems apparent that the short-lived pleasures of pot don't contribute anything of lasting value to a healthy lifestyle. Smoking marijuana is a risk to permanent and long-term good health.

Cocaine and the Workplace

In the last few years, the media has been full of stories about well-known athletes and entertainers who use cocaine. John Belushi is one famous example of a user who didn't survive his addiction to this popular drug. The facts of cocaine's dangers haven't quite infiltrated the consciousness of America yet; its use among young adults has tripled during the past few years.

Cocaine is one of the most powerful and seductive drugs in use today. The drug shares many of the same side effects as marijuana, LSD, PCP, uppers, and downers—none of them good. Its addictive qualities are some of its most hazardous.

In the February 18, 1985 issue of *Business Week,* a manager in a California electronics plant and former chronic cocaine user himself reported that 60 percent of his employees used cocaine regularly. "They are lucky to work ten days in a row," he said. "We probably lose $1,500 a week just in drug-related absenteeism."

A Los Angeles labor lawyer says that his work with drug-related problems has "tripled or quadrupled in the last few years."

In an attempt to stop the spread of employee drug abuse, IBM revealed that all potential new employees, from janitors to vice presidents, must pass a urinalysis test before they can be hired. "IBM's decision," says a high-tech executive, "is a milestone for the industry. No doubt other companies will follow suit."

Getting Help

Cocaine is not the stuff of dreams; it is the stuff of nightmares. People who figure they'll try anything once may not get a second chance. Almost everyone knows of someone who has waged a battle against addiction, whether it's a well-known athlete, a celebrity, or a friend. Fortunately, there are many fine treatment centers to assist in this awesome battle. Thousands of others have turned to professional hospitals like the Betty Ford Clinic for expert help.

The unfortunate fact of cocaine is that people who don't seek help most often lose the war against this powerful drug. As you evaluate your attitude toward cocaine, remember that no one *plans* to become an addict. And no one can become one without trying the drug at least once. For more information on addiction, prevention, and intervention, call the National Cocaine Hotline at 800-COCAINE.

The most successful drug rehabilitation program that I'm aware of in the nation is Teen Challenge, established by Dave Wilkerson. His best-selling book, *The Cross and the Switchblade*, tells how he began his work among the drug addicts of New York City.

Most major cities have a Teen Challenge center where anyone can receive the help and support they need to kick the drug habit. For more information contact Teen Challenge.

Medicating our aches and pains with drugs never solves the real problem. Even prescription drugs can be harmful when abused. Illicit drugs may be a temptation to teens who are subjected to peer pressure, professional athletes who are suddenly catapulted into a higher income bracket, or executives who have extra discretionary income.

If you're on drugs, *stop.* Programs are available to help you break your addiction. If you're not taking drugs, *don't start.* You'll be saving yourself pain, money, and a criminal record if you're caught buying, selling, or possessing illegal substances. Best of all, you'll be adding years to your life.

5

Slow Motion Suicide

"Cigarette smoking is the single most important environmental factor contributing to premature mortality in the United States," says the Department of Health, Education, and Welfare.

Smoking is slow-motion suicide. As the largest preventable cause of death in America, it is the number one risk factor.

All the data points in that direction. C. Norman Shealy, M.D., Ph.D. says, "[Smoking] contributes to more illness, disease, and premature death than all other risk factors put together."

Ready to Quit?

Smoking has gotten a lot of bad press the past several years, and rightfully so. A woman in one of my seminars said, "I've read so much about the negative effects of smoking, I've decided to quit—reading!"

I won't bore you with details. Some new facts, however, may further emphasize the importance of controlling this destructive habit.

When we inhale carbon monoxide, it attaches itself to red blood cells, preventing oxygen from being transported via the bloodstream in sufficient amounts. The result is mild to severe oxygen starvation of vital organs in the body, including the heart. Cigarette smoking causes the heart to beat faster—up to 10,000 extra times each day. This starvation on a cellular level is the primary cause of premature aging throughout the body.

We already know that smoking is the number one cause of lung cancer. But it's also true that a two-pack-a-day smoker is twenty times more likely to die of lung cancer than a nonsmoker. It causes a premature death every eighty-seven seconds—approximately 1,000 per day and nearly 365,000 each year. It is estimated that the time spent smoking equals the time reduced from life expectancy.

Hot Facts About Smoking

Let's look at some of the facts about this dangerous habit.

- Smoking contributes to nearly 365,000 deaths each year.
- The number one cause of lung cancer is smoking.
- Smokers increase their risk of stroke 20 percent.
- Seventy-seven million work days are lost each year because of smoking.
- Ten percent of all hospital and medical expenses in the U.S. are tobacco related.
- An employer spends $1000 to $5000 more per year to employ a smoker than a nonsmoker.
- Absenteeism rates are one-third to one-half higher for smokers than nonsmokers.

I'm reminded of a sign in a hotel room that read, "Don't smoke in bed. The ashes that fall on the floor may be your own."

Smoking is costly. Not only does it cost to purchase cigarettes and replace soiled or burned clothing and property, it is the cause of expensive and unnecessary illness, disease, and accidental death.

Internal Medicine News reported that analysis of 595 automobile crashes showed that smoking drivers are 50 percent more likely to cause accidents than nonsmokers. Accidents are caused by searching for cigarettes or a light, lighting up, smoke fogging on windshields, eye irritations, coughing fits, and hot ashes on clothes or car.

A smoker has an average of 30 to 40 percent less vitamin C in their bloodstreams than nonsmokers, which severely reduces their immune system's natural defenses. In addition to the costs we've already discussed, you can tack on about three dollars per pack to battle the lung cancer, emphysema, and coronary artery disease that it causes.

Smoking may cause or aggravate:

- Chronic bronchitis
- Emphysema
- High cholesterol
- Lung cancer
- High blood pressure
- Atherosclerosis
- Coronary heart disease
- Stroke

The good news is that when someone stops smoking, the body immediately begins the regenerative process. It will actually heal itself—especially the lungs. Within seven years, the lungs can recover to their normal state—unless the body has already developed cancer.

Smoke in the Workplace

The cost of cigarette smoking to business is high as well. Over 77 million work days are lost each year due to the effects of smoking. Business now spends over 50 billion dollars a year on medical care, accidents, lost productivity, and absenteeism.

Absenteeism rates average one-third higher for smokers because smoking severely reduces the effectiveness of the smoker's natural immune system. Few employers realize that smoking employees can cost them up to $5000 more per year than nonsmokers.

Two-thirds of the smoke from a burning cigarette go into the environment. This smoke has twice the nicotine, five times the carbon monoxide, and fifty times the ammonia as the smoke that is directly inhaled. When smokers smoke, the people around them smoke, too. Annually, between 500 to 5,000 nonsmokers will die from lung cancer as a result of other people's smoke.

If you're concerned about the problem and would like to begin a campaign in your company to eliminate smoking, perhaps these suggestions will help:

1. Establish support for a no-smoking policy. Involve members of top management.

2. Provide educational literature to employees.

3. Form a task force composed of diverse areas and management. Include at least one individual with research skills.

4. Conduct a survey to inform employees that the topic is being examined. You'll gather valuable data about your employee population.

5. Establish a no-smoking policy. Begin educating and informing employees through a well-formed publicity campaign. Put up no-smoking signs, and offer information sessions.

6. Offer a "stop smoking" program. You may decide to give bonuses or incentives. Perhaps give small monetary bonuses to nonsmokers, and offer smokers the same rewards if they give up smoking for six months.

7. Phase in restrictions gradually. Employees react more positively to changes when given time to adjust.

8. Deal with militant smokers. Smoking is a privilege not a right that is subject to other company rules. (Employees aren't allowed to listen to radios full blast, for instance.)

9. Be flexible. You may decide to make adjustments in the program.

Smoking: Hazardous to Your Career?

According to Robert Half International, nonsmokers are much more likely to hold top jobs. The old image of a hard-working, chain-smoking executive is out. In fact, a survey of America's one hundred largest corporations shows the vast majority of top executives are nonsmokers; 61 percent of those executives have successfully kicked the habit.

Prospective employees who smoke are increasingly being shunned by employers. Given a choice between two applicants who are equally qualified, rarely will the smoker be chosen over the nonsmoker.

Robert Rosner, a Seattle-based consultant to executives on how to run "healthier" businesses, is convinced it has clearly become an issue of economics.

A prime example is one of his clients who got a $6,000-a-year rebate from its janitorial service after instituting a no-smoking policy. The service reported that it required much less time and material to clean windows, furniture, and rugs in a smoke-free office.

Rosner reports, "Smokers are seen as a drain on the company ledgers." Obviously, smoking is becoming increasingly hazardous to one's career.

How Smoking Affects Women and Their Children

Over the past few years the number of men who smoke has declined, and the number of women smokers has remained about the same (rather than increasing dramatically as it had been previously). Unfortunately, the number of young women and teenage girls who smoke is on the rise—an especially sad fact because of the effects of smoking during child-bearing years.

Lung cancer in women has increased nearly 350 percent since 1950. It has surpassed breast cancer as the leading cause of cancer deaths.

The children of smokers suffer the effects of smoking without ever picking up a cigarette. Without their consent, children and even unborn babies are directly affected.

Smoking can increase the risk of miscarriage or stillbirth by about 50 percent. It can also be responsible for premature birth, low birth weight (the leading cause of death in the first year of life), birth defects, death in infancy, difficult breathing in infancy, learning problems later in school, and a predisposition toward anxiety.

Smoking and Pregnancy

Pregnant women who smoke may be doing irreparable damage to their unborn children. A fetus depends on its mother for full-term nourishment and healthy gestation. When a pregnant woman smokes, she subjects her baby to the serious effects of nicotine and carbon monoxide.

Nicotine tightens blood vessels and restricts the quantity and quality of oxygen to the fetus. It also increases blood pressure in both the mother and baby. Nursing babies actually consume nicotine from breast milk!

In the book *The Secret Life of the Unborn Child* by Thomas Verny, M.D. and John Kelly, a study conducted by Dr. Michael Lieberman is discussed that showed how unborn children grow emotionally agitated each time their mother even *thinks* of having a cigarette. This agitation is evidenced by a quickening of the child's heartbeat.

The unborn child experiences mild to severe physical discomfort due to the reduction of his or her flow of oxygen each time the mother smokes. The unborn child never knows when this unpleasant sensation will occur or how painful it will be when it occurs—only that it will reoccur. She or he eventually becomes chronically uncertain and fearful. This conditioned state stays with the child and can lead to deep-seated anxiety.

Setting a Good Example

When parents smoke, their children are likely to have twice as many colds and respiratory problems as the children of nonsmokers. Their chances of being smaller and shorter than other children is increased. They will also be twice as likely to become smokers as the children of non-smokers.

A number of years ago, a television commercial accurately showed the impact that smoking parents have on their children. A man and his young son were walking and playing beside a lake. When the father kicked a leaf, the son kicked a leaf. When the father skipped a stone across the lake, the boy did the same. Then they leaned against a tree to rest. The father took out a pack of cigarettes, lit one, inhaled, and set the pack on the ground. As the father gazed reflectively over the lake, the son reached down to pick up the pack and pull out a cigarette. What kind of role models are we?

Teenagers, especially, are tempted to smoke. Often they are not as aware of the serious hazards of smoking. Parents and teachers must be able to discuss the issue and encourage self-esteem-building activities such as sports, music, recreation, and scholastic achievements.

Role-modeling is consistently the strongest influence on behavior. The golden chance to teach our vulnerable youth cannot be achieved as effectively through any other method. A parent's opportunity to teach their children cannot be accomplished by pushing, pulling, or pointing the way nearly as well as by *showing* the way. Anyone can learn a lesson from a good example.

You Can Stop Smoking

Yes, smoking is the number one health risk in our society. It contributes to more illness, disease, and premature death than all other risk factors combined. One philosophy holds that man was put on this earth to suffer—and the tobacco industry was put here to see that he does.

Most smokers smoke more when they're tense. It helps them relax, they say. Smoking *is* calming to a point. The smoker's body has come to depend on nicotine, and smoking satisfies a craving. But this restoration of the nicotine level is only temporary relief. Once in the body, nicotine *stimulates* the heart and increases blood pressure. As a way of managing tension, smoking is counterproductive. Several slow breaths, especially through the nose, are much more effective.

Despite their physical need to smoke, I believe that most of the 54 million smokers in the United States would like to quit. For the most part, they know the consequences of their actions. But quitting is easier said than done. I know. I didn't quit on my first try.

Mark Twain said, "To cease smoking is the easiest thing I ever did. I ought to know because I've done it a thousand times."

Keep trying, and you will succeed. Try every method. Don't give up. The process you use to stop is secondary to the result. You can quit. Over 50 million others have, and the number is growing.

Changing Your Lifestyle

The most powerful adjunct to any stop-smoking campaign is exercise. Next are water, fruits, and vegetables. All help-rid the body of poisonous toxins and the craving for cigarettes.

If you are a smoker and you want to lower your risk of smoking related illnesses, here are several lifestyle changes you will want to make:

- Exercise
- Stop smoking
- Manage stress
- Reduce fast-forward, Type "A" attitudes
- Eat a healthy diet

As soon as you stop smoking (unless you have already developed cancer), your body will begin to heal itself. Your risk of lung cancer is virtually eliminated and your risk of heart disease is reduced measurably.

Living with Emphysema

In addition to all the research available, I am personally familiar with the devastating effect smoking has on health.

My mother-in-law, Jane, had been smoking for about forty-three years when, two years ago, her doctor diagnosed her chronic coughing and shortness of breath as emphysema. After testing, he concluded that she had 25 percent capacity in one lung and 10 percent capacity in the other.

Due to the severity of her condition, the doctor put Jane on oxygen twenty-four hours a day. Usually an emphysema patient requires oxygen only a few hours a day during the early stages of the disease.

Before Jane started experiencing the symptoms that led to her oxygen treatment, she had been an extremely active individual. People used to wonder where she got her energy, and she was considered to be somewhat of a matriarch in her family. Jane was the one everyone came to for help.

Today Jane can only walk thirty feet across a room with a walker—and that is on a good day. Her good days are made possible, in part, by the numerous medications she takes, which cost approximately $350 per month. Some of these medications treat the symptoms of emphysema. Others are necessary to assist her with the many bodily dysfunctions she experiences as a result of the disease. Additional medications are needed to counteract the side-effects of all the medications she is taking.

Shattered Dreams

Jane has made five emergency trips to the hospital during the past twelve months. It is becoming apparent that she needs constant care with consistent medical intervention. Jane's family is doing as much as they can to provide the constant care, medical attention, love, and support that she needs while still managing their own lives.

Roy, Jane's husband, seems to be having the hardest time emotionally adjusting to his wife's illness. They have been married for fifty years. He is very disappointed at having to give up his dream of sharing their well-deserved "golden years" together.

In addition, Roy is somewhat helpless to stop the steady depletion of their financial resources as the bill for doctors, hospitals, nursing care, and miscellaneous medical expenses mount. Even though he and Jane worked extremely hard over the years to escape from poverty during the depression and built a solid financial position, they may very well lose everything in the process of paying for these medical expenses.

Don't Ever Start

The sad reality of this situation is that it could have been prevented. If Jane could have foreseen the pain, frustration, cost, and destruction smoking would ultimately cause her and her family, she would never have started smoking.

My mother, Carol, who is now sixty-five years old, tried to quit smoking many times, but her attempts had always failed—until recently. After forty-five years as a smoker, she hasn't had a cigarette in over fourteen weeks. If she can quit, anyone can.

In a recent conversation with her, I asked if there was any advice she would give to the readers of this book about smoking. She said, "Just three words: *Don't ever start!*"

We have an obligation first to our Creator, then to ourselves, and then to our families to take care of our health. If we don't, they could very well pay an unnecessary price right along with us.

6
The Socially-Accepted Killer

America's most abused substance is not marijuana, cocaine, or any other drug—it is alcohol. The average person drinks nearly three gallons of alcohol every year.

Because drinking alcohol has become a socially-acceptable pastime—and because we tend to view it as a compulsory activity—liquor is nearly always present at gatherings of celebration. Alcohol is found at weddings, New Years' parties, restaurants, and business luncheons.

We have been culturally indoctrinated; as a result we tend to minimize its risks. But let's look at the facts:

- Alcohol is a factor in one out of every ten deaths in the U.S.
- Every twenty-three minutes someone dies from an alcohol-related incident.
- Alcohol is connected with:
  - 50 percent of all automobile fatalities
  - 80 percent of all home violence
  - 30 percent of all suicides
  - 60 percent of all child abuse
  - 50 percent of all homicides

Alcohol contributes directly to liver cirrhosis, which ranks sixth in the listing of common causes of death. Alcohol is a deadly drug.

Who are the Problem Drinkers?

Let's look at the statistics concerning problem drinkers.

- One out of every ten people in the U.S. becomes a problem drinker or alcoholic.
- 28 percent of adult male drinkers and 8 percent of female drinkers are classified as heavy drinkers.
- Married females working outside the home have "significantly higher" rates of problem drinking than do other women.
- 15 percent of teen-aged drinkers consume 5 or more drinks at a time, at least once a week.
- 85 percent of the problem drinkers and alcoholics are *not* getting formal treatment.

The costs of alcohol abuse to businesses are horrendous. In his book, *The Courage To Change*, Dennis Wholey reports that employers lose over 65 billion dollars annually in lost production, absenteeism, property damage, and health and medical services.

In a 1982 Congressional report, the report's principal author, Leonard Saxon at Boston University, says, "The cost of alcoholism and alcohol abuse in the U.S. today is estimated to be 120 billion dollars." That's 120 *billion*.

What Makes People Drink?

Alcohol may be relaxing and enjoyable if used properly. There has even been some research showing that drinking in moderation can reduce the risk of heart disease. It may even enhance longevity. But for an individual with even the slightest tendency toward a drinking problem, the risks far outweigh the benefits of drinking any alcoholic beverage.

Several factors may aggravate alcohol abuse and alcoholism:

- Excessive stress
- Depression
- Gatherings where alcohol is the main attraction
- Financial difficulties
- Personal-family crisis
- Job dissatisfaction
- Heredity
- Fast-forward, Type "A" attitudes

As with any destructive lifestyle pattern, the choices we make have the greatest impact on whether we are going to let anything take control of our lives.

Worth the Risk?

The risks involved in a life of problem drinking far outweigh a few moments of light-hearted pleasure. Alcohol abuse and alcoholism may cause or aggravate:

- Cirrhosis of the liver
- Brain atrophy
- Some forms of cancer
- Pneumonia
- Birth defects
- Motor vehicle accidents
- High blood pressure
- Stroke
- Homicide
- Suicide
- Premature death

Drinking too much can also contribute to low self-esteem, job loss, family and marital problems, and financial losses to business. Is it worth it?

Alcohol and Pregnancy

Alcohol poses additional risks during pregnancy. Alcohol accumulates and remains in the unborn child's system much longer than it does in the mother's. The developing liver in the baby cannot cleanse its bloodstream of alcohol as well as the mother's can. In fact, the infant can actually be born addicted to alcohol and undergo withdrawal.

In 1978, the National Insurance on Alcohol Abuse and Alcoholism (NIAAA), announced that one ounce of pure alcohol per day would be the healthy limit of liquor for pregnant women. That equals two mixed drinks, two five-ounce glasses of wine, or two twelve-ounce beers. Now, because of the danger involved in even low level alcohol consumption, the NIAAA suggests that pregnant women not drink at all.

Because a baby's protective mechanisms are not mature, the drink taken by an expectant mother is also, literally, taken by the baby. If an expectant mother gets drunk, so does the baby. And although the physical effects of alcohol are short-term, they count toward an increased risk of miscarriage and premature birth.

Fetal Alcohol Syndrome

An additional risk, fetal alcohol syndrome (FAS) is the third leading cause of mental retardation among newborns. It occurs in babies of pregnant women who drink regularly, moderately, or excessively. The fast-growing tissues of the unborn, especially the brain, cannot withstand the effects of this intoxication.

After birth, the child will have a combination of physical, mental, and behavioral problems as a result of a smaller brain and impairment of the central nervous system. Behavior disorders may include hyperactivity, short attention span, sleep disturbance, and mild to moderate mental retardation. Affected babies are abnormally small at birth in both height and weight, and are poorly coordinated (a problem that will persist as the child develops). Almost 50 percent of all FAS babies are born with heart defects.

In many cases, FAS babies look like each other rather than their parents. They share some common characteristics, including small head size, narrow eyes, a short, upturned nose, a thin upper lip, under-developed skin between the lip and nose, and flat facial features.

A pregnant woman who drinks may or may not have a baby affected by fetal alcohol syndrome. But a woman who does not drink at all while pregnant is guaranteed that her baby will not experience it.

The data about alcohol-related illness is shocking. My intent is not to frighten you, but I do want to present the facts that are available. Then you can weigh the risks and make wise choices.

Are You a Problem Drinker?

It is my personal concern that everyone who needs help should get it. The following questions should be asked if you're considering whether or not you drink too much alcohol. If your answer is "yes" to most of the questions below, please seek help for a more in-depth, professional evaluation.

1. Do you drink in the early morning?
2. Do you drink alone?
3. Do you drink when you're bored and lonely?
4. Do you lose time from work as a result of your alcohol consumption?
5. Do you experience blackouts or amnesia when you have been drinking?

6. Have you been experiencing mood changes?

7. Are you losing ambition and efficiency?

8. Are you worrying your family or harming them in any way as a result of your drinking?

9. Do you require medical treatment for symptoms related to your drinking?

10. Do you need a drink to relax?

11. Do you often drink to get drunk?

During the past decade, substantial steps have been made toward understanding and treating the alcohol disease. As a result of a new awareness of the seriousness and extent of alcoholism in our society, treatment systems are appearing in burgeoning numbers.

Motivated by the realization that alcoholism is more expensive to let slide than to treat, business leaders all over the nation are sponsoring treatment programs for their employees. Presently, more than 50 percent of *Fortune* magazine's top 500 companies offer occupational alcohol disease treatment programs. Prevention of alcohol abuse and alcoholism through education and early treatment are the best alternatives now and for the future.

Lifestyle Choices You Can Make

There are several lifestyle changes you can make to help lower your risk of alcohol abuse and alcoholism:

- Abstain from drinking alcohol in any form
- Limit your intake if you do drink
- Avoid mixing alcohol and drugs
- Avoid drinking situations
- Do not drink and drive
- Do not permit drinking friends to drive
- Educate yourself about alcoholism by contacting Alcoholics Anonymous or Alanon (for families of the alcoholic)

Overshadowed by Alcohol

People tell me that it's not the first drink that gets you— it's the ones that follow. I question that logic. If you get hit by a train, what kills you? The engine or the caboose?

That little analogy reminded me of my father and the fact that he worked on the railroad, primarily as a fireman and engineer for approximately thirty-two years. He was touted by his peers to be one of, if not *the* best hoghead (engineer) of his time.

At age nineteen my dad served his country in World War II as a platoon sergeant with the highly decorated 164th Infantry in Guadalcanal, South Pacific.

Dad was also a great athlete. He would have been inducted into the North Dakota Softball Hall of Fame if he had filled out the paperwork. Then in the late 1950s, he won the North Dakota state bowling championship, averaging 206 per game.

Obviously, my father had many talents. He was also an intelligent, sensitive person. Unfortunately, all of these fine qualities, including his attempt to be the kind of husband and father he really wanted to be, were overshadowed and negatively influenced by his addiction to alcohol.

My father completed several alcoholism rehabilitation programs and at one time remained sober for six years. Although he struggled to win the war with alcohol, our family was destroyed. My parents were divorced after twenty-two years of a "marriage on the rocks." My father ruined his health and died prematurely at the age of fifty-six, having lost the war with alcoholism.

What Could Have Been

Due to the many painful experiences my family had as a result of living with an alcoholic, I must admit there were few good times as a *family*. But I feel that because of the stability and sanity that my mother brought to the family, my brother, two sisters, and I have been able to use these negative experiences to our advantage rather than to our disadvantage in most instances.

I'm not sure how my mom was able to sustain her own well-being and have anything left over for us children, but she did. In a recent conversation with her, she told me that her strength came from having a healthy family foundation when she was growing up. Through supportive encouragement from her parents and family, she had acquired a strong self-worth and a belief in God. She had a solid enough foundation to weather her stormy twenty-two-year marriage and still be a responsible mother to her four children.

Sometimes when I think about my father, I miss him and think of what he could have been, what he should have been, what he missed, what we missed, what if—knowing full well that what could, should, and what if will never be.

Even so, if Dad were here, I would want him to know that in spite of everything, I love him.

Help for the Alcoholic

The only possible explanation I can offer to myself as to the origin of my father's bondage to alcohol is a combination of his family history, a genetic predisposition to alcoholism, and the memories he carried with him from the war. However, the origins of the pain we experience, no matter how heinous, don't necessarily doom us to alcoholism or any other destructive behavior. Our response to life's pain is within our power to choose.

I believe that when we are confronted with an addiction as horrendous as alcoholism, our best hope is to pray honestly and earnestly for deliverance. Alcoholics Anonymous was founded on the principle that alcoholics are powerless over alcohol. Alcoholics Anonymous also has a philosophy that God can and will help them cope with their problems if they demonstrate a desire to stop drinking by not taking that first drink.

I do not know if Dad prayed honestly or earnestly for deliverance. But I hope that he did not suffer completely alone. I hope that in his struggle he called on the Lord for strength. The fact that he died in bondage to alcohol does not mean that he didn't or that he is lost eternally. The only thing it means is that he did not gain victory over this most formidable foe.

Alcohol is dangerous, destructive, and deadly. It is dangerous like fire—the longer you play with it the more likely you are to get burned. It is destructive, as it was the major contributing factor to the break up of my parents' marriage and our family. It is deadly, as our family learned, when Dad died at an age that could have been his "prime time."

Families of alcoholics also need counseling and help. Toby Rice Drew's book, *Getting Them Sober: A Guide for Those who Live with an Alcoholic* provides excellent advice for wives and children trying to deal with a problem drinker in the family.

What Does God Say About It?

Before moving on to other subjects, let's consider what God says about drugs and alcohol. The Bible is not silent on this subject, as the following scripture proves.

> Wine is a mocker and beer a brawler; whoever is led astray by them is not wise—Proverbs 20:1, NIV.

God still looks upon taking "recreational" drugs and drinking to excess as sin. In Ephesians 5:18, the apostle Paul says, "Do not get drunk on wine, which leads to debauchery. Instead, be filled with the Spirit" (NIV). The Lord wants us to be prosperous, happy, and content, but He doesn't want us to depend on chemicals or false highs. *He* wants to be the source of our joy.

Unhealthy behavioral patterns can severely affect our general good health, whether they are related to drugs, alcohol, smoking, or eating disorders. Ironically, the individual involved resorts to them in order to alleviate or sooth anxiety, pressure, and low self-esteem—and these activities do nothing to help correct these problems. Instead, they may aggravate them. The original problems remain intact. At best, we've only masked or prolonged them.

The goal of high performance individuals is to avoid what hinders them and make responsible use of what helps them. In the next few chapters, we will discuss the best physical antidote for a destructive lifestyle.

Part Two

Making Changes for Better Living

7

Eating to Live?
Or Living to Eat?

When I was growing up, my primary motivation for eating was to give my mouth a good time. I think we're trained to do that. It follows that fun, satisfaction, and reward are the primary motivating factors behind adult eating habits.

But eating foods lacking nutritive value is like polishing your car when it's out of gas. You'll feel great sitting inside that shiny car, but you won't get anywhere until you put in the fuel.

Why do Americans have unhealthy eating habits? Why are so many deaths linked to our diets? Why don't more people live to be one hundred and beyond? And why don't we eat the proper foods in the correct amounts? Because too often we eat for the wrong reasons.

Emotional Eating

Our primary reason for eating has become emotional. We eat for reward, pleasure, and "because it's time."

Around lunchtime I like to ask people, "Are you hungry?" The way they respond always amazes me. Most of them will look at their watch to find the answer!

Eating to provide our bodies with the vital fuel for our biological-human machines—i.e., bodies—has become our secondary motivation. Instead, we eat almost exclusively for pleasure, often neglecting our bodies' fuel needs.

Eating for emotional reasons will have temporary rewards, but it will do little to help you function at your best. It will, in fact, take its toll.

Because many people have this emotional attachment to food, they eat or don't eat for the wrong reasons. As a result eating disorders have caused countless numbers of people great anguish.

Many health care professionals believe that the greatest health problem in our society today is the unhealthy use of food. Later we will find out about patterns of healthy nutrition and eating, but now let's concern ourselves with how the misuse of food can be destructive.

Compulsive Overeating

There are many levels of eating disorders. The most common is *compulsive overeating,* the habit that causes bulges and additional poundage—the penalty for exceeding the "feed limit." Habitual overeating may lead to compulsive overeating, which is an "addiction" to food.

Because our primary motivations behind eating are reward and pleasure, it's easy to see how we develop bad habits that lead to food abuse. Food often is used as a reward while we are growing up. A bag of chips, a candy bar, or a second serving pacifies us for the moment. But its effects, like a drug, only make us feel better temporarily. A food reward doesn't have any long-term benefits and may, in fact, aggravate the real problem.

In her book, *The Diet Alternative*, Diane Hampton describes her battle with compulsive overeating:

Once I gained thirty pounds in three months. **Food was on my mind constantly. When I woke** up in the morning, my first thoughts were about what I would eat that day. I wondered if I would be able to control my eating at all, or if I would succumb to my desire to gorge. Even when I was on one of my frequent diets . . . I was obsessed with thoughts of food. I was also usually depressed.

I read every diet and weight control book I could find. I tried "self-hypnosis." I went to a physician for hypnosis. I went to a psychologist. I even went to a weight doctor. But there was something inside me that continued to drive me to overeat.

Diane goes on to tell how the Lord delivered her from the *sin* of overeating. Today, her seminars on *Scriptural Eating Patterns* are helping thousands of people experience freedom from the bondage to food. For information about seminars or audio tapes write to: Scriptural Living Ministries, 2031 Creekpoint Drive, St. Peters, Missouri 63376, (314) 441-4245.

Anorexia Nervosa

The fear of food can lead to another eating disorder—*anorexia nervosa*. People who are afflicted literally starve themselves to death. About one in every 200 women and one in every 2000 men are anorexic. Two of the best known anorexic victims are Cherry Boone O'Neill and Karen Carpenter. Both received professional help. Karen didn't survive the effects anorexia had on her body. Cherry has done well since treatment and has become a mother. She has written a book about her experience called *Starving For Attention*.

I have a good friend who a few years ago was diagnosed as anorexic; to preserve her anonymity, I'll call her Doris.

I met her while she was working in a management position with a large national company.

The first two or three years after we became acquainted, we corresponded between cities and communicated frequently by telephone. Our conversations were casual and constructive. Doris was always prompt in returning my calls and correspondence.

Suddenly her calls and letters became sporadic. Many times, after leaving a message, I wouldn't hear from her at all.

Other professional associates also noticed the change. "Have you talked to Doris lately?" everyone was asking. Typically the answer was "No, I left a message for her, but she hasn't gotten back to me yet." As time passed, our feelings fluctuated between frustration, disappointment, rejection, anger, and concern.

The incident that really got my attention occurred while I was under contract with the company that employed Doris. I was in an East coast city presenting a seminar at an annual conference. As Doris had always been an avid supporter of my work, I expected to see her. She never showed up. Her co-workers told me that "something came up."

Upon the conclusion of the conference we returned to Doris's facility, where I was scheduled to conduct an informal training session. I was happy to hear that Doris was in and hurried to her office.

When I saw her, I was shocked. She had always been on the thin side and preoccupied with her appearance, but today she reminded me of pictures I had seen of concentration camp survivors. The only difference was that she was smartly dressed and well-groomed. I gave her a hug. She was skin and bones. A few months later I heard from one of her peers that she had lost still more weight. She was down to seventy-five pounds. It was slow motion suicide.

The problem with this illness is that its sufferers don't always believe they are sick. Unless they get professional help, anorexic patients may become part of the 10-15 percent who die of the disease. By the way, Doris did get help, and she is healthier today than she's ever been.

Bulimia

A related eating disorder, *bulimia* is also a fear of food, but it causes its victims to binge on food regularly. In their never-ending battle to remain thin, they take laxatives and force themselves to vomit. About one in 80 women and one in every 400 men are bulimic. One million Americans suffer from these disorders, and 150,000 people die each year as a result.

It's easy for us to turn away from individuals who suffer from eating disorders because often they turn away from us, reject us, avoid us, and withdraw from us. But we must be there and continue to love them. We must, in fact, love them enough to take whatever course of action is necessary to get them professional help—even when it hurts. We must be willing to become involved.

Today there are many fine treatment centers available as well as professionals who understand these complex eating-related illnesses. Contact a health professional or check your local telephone directory for referrals.

Inherited Habits

I often wonder if the habits we inherit are more destructive than the genes we inherit. Many of our present lifestyle habits were formed during the formative years of childhood. How many of you who were told to "clean off your plate" are still cleaning off your plates today?

Take time to evaluate how many habits you still have from those early years. These learned habits could be eating, drinking, smoking, exercising, watching TV, or other behaviors that have developed from imitating other people.

A growing number of health professionals believe that learned hereditary habits play a key role in raising or lowering our vulnerability to the degenerative diseases in our modern day civilization. Current evidence shows that more than 50 percent of the most common causes of death are due to the way we live—our lifestyles learned from family, friends, and role models.

Overfed and Undernourished

Dr. Charles Mayo said, "Let me repeat one solemn truth which should be repeated over and over each day until everybody comprehends its meaning and acts upon it . . . Normal resistance to disease is directly dependent upon adequate food."

Ours is the richest, best-fed nation on earth. Yet 60 percent of the leading causes of death in the United States are diet-related. We export hundreds of thousands of pounds of produce to the world's hungry, yet we remain undernourished even though we overeat. How can this be?

Most people don't eat the proper foods in the correct amounts or in the most healthful ways. Everything we eat either increases or decreases energy and our ability to manage the demands placed upon our bodies. The effects of poorly managed stress and our overall health can be decreased or increased by the types of food we eat.

In a report called "Dietary Goals for the U.S.," the U.S. Senate Select Committee on Nutrition and Human Needs made the following statement:

> Our diets have changed radically over the last 50 years, with great and often very harmful effects on our health. These dietary changes represent as great a threat to public health as smoking. Too much fat, too much sugar and salt, can be and are linked directly to killer diseases such as heart disease, cancer, stroke, and diabetes. In all, six of the leading ten causes of death in the U.S. have been linked to our diet.

What's Wrong with Potato Chips?

Our need to fill emotional rather than nutritional hungers often leads us to reach for over-processed and unbalanced foods. Let's consider the potato chip. In its raw form, the potato is exceptionally high in nutrients. But it undergoes a change between the earth and the airtight bag. The outer edge of the potato (just under the peel), with its high concentration of nutrients, is peeled away. The remaining potato is cut into thin pieces, soaked in preservatives, and cooked in oils that contain no nutritive value.

A handful of these treats contain about one hundred calories; and they are saturated with fats and chemicals our bodies cannot metabolize. After cooking, the chips are heavily salted. Salt is a non-food that has a corrosive effect on the body's vitamin supplies.

Salt forces potassium out of the body. This changes the delicate acid-base balance of our nerve cells and tissues. Over time, this imbalance can influence the electrical impulses of our nervous system, which, in turn, affects the heart, blood pressure, and circulatory system, as well as other systems of the body.

All this from potato chips. Why does our nation consume millions of pounds of them every year, if we know all about their lack of nutritive value? Because they fill an emotional need. They taste good, and they're accessible.

A Move in the Wrong Direction

If we were to reverse the order of our reasons for eating—if we were to eat first for fuel and nutrition and second for taste and pleasure—we could virtually eliminate the physical and psychological problems that are a direct result of poor nutrition.

Since the early 1900s, our westernized diet has changed greatly. We eat fewer fresh vegetables, fruits, and cereals. We eat much more refined flour, animal fats, salt, and sugar.

This change for the worse creates a higher incidence of "lifestyle diseases"—including cancer, hypertension, diabetes, arthritis, heart disease, and cirrhosis of the liver. The further we move from the natural food chain, the greater our risk of contracting lifestyle diseases.

Digging Your Grave with Your Fork?

Aside from the eating disorders we have mentioned in this chapter, there is a life-threatening disease that is directly related to overeating and poor eating habits. It is the third greatest killer in America. You may be surprised to learn that it is diabetes. Let's look at the facts:

- Over 10 million Americans suffer from diabetes. (Two-fifths or more don't know they have it.)
- Over 600,000 Americans learn they have diabetes each year.
- The average American has two to five odds of developing diabetes.
- Diabetes is the *third greatest killer* in America.
- Diabetics have at least two and a half times greater chance of *heart attack* and *stroke*.
- Diabetics are over five times more prone to gangrene (often leading to amputation).
- Diabetes *decreases life expectancy* by about one-third.
- Diabetics are seventeen times more prone to *kidney disease.*
- Diabetics are 25 percent more prone to *blindness.*

If you don't think diabetes is a serious disease, look at this list of consequences. Diabetes may cause or aggravate:

- High blood pressure
- Atherosclerosis

- Vascular disease
- Psychological complications
- Stroke
- Heart failure
- Kidney disease
- Gangrene
- Blindness
- Tuberculosis
- Premature Death

This disease of the pancreas prevents the body from making use of sugars and starches in a normal way. Problems occur when the pancreas does not produce enough insulin or the body cannot properly use the insulin it produces. The result is excess glucose.

This forces the body to draw upon fats and proteins for energy because there is not enough insulin or it is not interacting properly with the glucose to produce the energy it needs. The result is extreme fatigue.

There are basically two types of diabetes. The *insulindependent* is the most serious and accounts for about 10 percent of the cases. The pancreas produces little or no insulin on its own, and as a result the person becomes dependent on insulin from an external source. Although the insulin-dependent symptoms can occur at any age, they most often appear abruptly in children and in young adults who require immediate treatment.

The *non-insulin dependent* is the most common, the least serious, and accounts for 90 percent of the cases. The onset is usually slower and the symptoms are much more difficult to recognize than the insulin-dependent. Although non-insulin dependent diabetes can occur at any age, most cases do not occur until middle age or older and can usually be controlled with proper diet and exercise. In some cases oral medication may also be needed.

Some diabetics, especially those who are older, may experience few symptoms or none at all. But the following are the most common warning signals of diabetes:

- Frequent urination
- Excessive thirst
- Extreme hunger
- Rapid weight loss
- Drowsiness
- Easy tiring
- General weakness
- Blurred or change in vision
- Skin infections, boils, etc.

Are You at Risk?

Research shows a direct relationship between our susceptibility to certain diseases and our parents and grandparents. When you are conceived, the genetic structure transferred from your parents to you determines in many ways your ability to maintain health under the stress and strain of life.

Assuming that is true, let's look at the list below. Most of the factors mentioned are related to lifestyle and not heredity. You have a lot to say about the factors you are going to allow to influence your health.

Several factors may cause or aggravate diabetes:

- Unhealthy diet
- Overweight
- Over age 35
- High blood pressure
- Lack of exercise
- Poorly managed stress
- Fast-forward attitudes
- High cholesterol
- Heredity

Changing Your Ways

Diabetes is a disease to be avoided at all costs. Thank goodness there are several lifestyle changes you can make to lower your risk of diabetes.

- Lose weight (fat)
- Eat a healthy diet
- Control stress
- Exercise
- Reduce fast-forward attitudes
- Have a physical examination, including:
    Urine test
    Blood test
    Glucose tolerance test

In her book, *Are You Sick and Tired of Feeling Sick and Tired,* nutritionist Dr. Mary Ruth Swope says, "Statistics show that diabetes is *four times more common* in obese than in lean adults. A weight gain often precedes the *onset* of adult diabetes. As for adults who develop diabetes, she says "lowering body weight to normal and keeping it there eliminates the condition in many cases."

If food has become your enemy and you're eating for all the wrong reasons, it's time to get help. Your figure and appearance are not the only matters at stake. At far greater risk is your health and your life.

In the next few chapters, you'll discover how to eat right, how to lose weight, and how to keep it off.

8

Overweight or Overfat What's the Difference?

No one wants to be fat—at least no one I know. As a result of our fear of fat, we abuse our bodies in the pursuit of the elusive slim physique. And it *is* elusive, especially for women. Even if every woman was in good physical condition and the proper weight, less than 20 percent could be the perfect "10" because her genetic body structure wouldn't permit it.

While weight loss may not be the primary reason behind this book, it will be the natural result of creating a lifestyle you can live with. That lifestyle includes good eating habits and a reasonable amount of exercise. One of the most important factors related to weight loss is understanding the difference between overweight and overfat.

What is Overfat?

Overfat occurs when the percentage of body fat exceeds what is healthy for total body weight. Total body weight consists of all organs, glands, bones, muscles, and fat. All weight that is not fat is called *lean body mass,* or LBM.

The maximum healthy fat level for men is 15 percent; for women, it is 22 percent. A body in good physical condition—an athlete's for instance—normally has a much lower percentage of fat.

The most precise measure of LBM and body fat could be determined by taking a weight measurement under water. Because fat floats, the less the weight, the higher the percentage of fat. That is why it is difficult for lean people to float. (Overfat people float easily.)

A less accurate but obviously more practical method to determine LBM is to compare your acceptable weight for sex, height, and body build with your actual body weight. If you are within 10 percent of your recommended weight, and if you are exercising regularly, chances are good that your LBM and body fat ratio is within the desired range. Exercise significantly improves the likelihood of maintaining this healthy ratio. If you are not exercising consistently, your chances of having a healthy LBM-to-body fat ratio are poor.

What is Overweight?

A little boy was asked, "When you get as big as your dad, what will you do?" The little boy replied, "I'll go on a diet."

If you weigh more than is recommended for your sex, height, and body build, you are overweight. Obesity occurs when weight is 20 percent higher than the recommended weight.

According to the National Health Institute, over one-third of the United States population is obese. This is a dangerous state to be in. Obese persons—about 34 million in the United States—are at a high risk for a wide variety of diseases and illnesses, including high blood pressure, high blood cholesterol, adult-onset diabetes, cancer, heart disease, gall bladder disease, and many other problems.

Although total food consumption has decreased in the past ten years (10 percent for women, 15 percent for men), the average American today weighs as much as, or more than, the American of ten years ago. We have become more and more sedentary, which means that we burn less fuel (calories). We need to control our food intake and our use of it as well. And we need to regulate our natural tendency to become overfat and overweight.

Your Ideal Weight

Figure how much you should weigh. If you're left-handed, measure the left wrist. If you're right-handed, measure your right wrist.

Men of average bone size can multiply their height in inches times four and subtract 128. If the dominant wrist measures seven inches or larger, however, add 10 percent to the total. Women of average bone size can multiply their height in inches by 3.5 and subtract 108. If the dominant wrist measures 6 1/2'' or larger, add 10 percent to the total.

Example:
> 5' 11'' Man (71'') dominant wrist = 7''
> 71'' x 4 = 284 – 128 = 156 x 10% = 172 pounds
>
> 5' 6'' Woman (66'') dominant wrist = 6''
> 66'' x 3.5 = 231 – 108 = 123 pounds

Keep in mind that weight figures can be misleading. You could be overweight and even obese by the charts but not be overfat. Avid weight lifters and many football players fall into this category. The charts also do not take into account the decrease of muscle that normally occurs with age.

Many people aren't aware that as they grow older, the percentage of fat to LBM increases due to a drastic decrease (as high as 75 percent) in exercise. When people announce proudly that, ''I weigh the same as I did thirty years ago,'' they rarely consider how much of their weight is now fat rather than muscle.

Getting Back into Balance

When unhealthy eating patterns or habits are maintained for prolonged periods of time, the innate regulating system that tells us when, what, and how much to eat is forced out of balance. The system can be overridden so often that it adjusts to the persistent demand and establishes a new level or balance.

When this occurs, it is necessary to reevaluate eating patterns. It may also require an uncomfortable period of cutting back. Most likely, negative weight producing "tastes" will have to be avoided and natural dietary needs satisfied.

Overfat could be the result of glandular problems; your physician should be able to determine this. However, overweight (overfat) is almost always a result of faulty diet and lack of exercise.

Although the quantity and especially the quality of food that is habitually placed in the body should be carefully evaluated, the most potent weapon available to us in the battle of the bulge is not the four-letter word *diet*, but the eight-letter word that most people don't want to hear— *exercise*. We'll talk more about that later.

Crash Diets

Crash diets generally do more harm than good, making the dieter weak, irritable, and dizzy. They also rarely work. When they do, their effects usually last only a short time. In fact, the dieter usually regains the weight lost plus a few additional pounds.

The old adage is all too true: the best way to reduce is the same way the extra weight was put on—a pound at a time. Study after study has shown that those who reduce slowly and consistently by decreasing caloric intake and increasing the amount of exercise have a much greater likelihood of keeping off fat.

I am very skeptical of any fat (weight) reduction program that asks participants to consume less than 1,000 calories a day. I am also cautious of any program that promises miraculous fat loss.

Anytime a weight loss program is considered, these questions should be asked:

1. Is the program going to help me change my eating habits to keep the fat off?
2. Does the program advocate and promote the value of exercise?

When both questions can't be answered "yes," the program being considered is not a complete one.

Each pound of fatty tissue is equivalent in energy to about 3,500 calories. Every time we eat 3,500 calories less than we burn, we lose one pound of fatty tissue. When we eat 500 calories a day less than we burn, we lose one pound a week, or fifty-two pounds per year. If we eat 1,000 calories a day less than we burn, we take off two pounds per week—104 pounds a year.

How Your Body Gains Weight

Your body controls its fat (weight) level in a method similar to the one used by a thermostat to control heat. I'll call this innate mechanism a *fatostat*. Your body automatically adjusts its metabolism (furnace) to maintain the level set by the fatostat—usually within a range of five to ten pounds.

For an example of how this system works, think of a bear. In the fall, a bear's fatostat is set low—and remains turned down to this level throughout the hibernation period. When the fatostat is turned down to maintain a high fat level, the body metabolism remains low, enabling the bear to burn fat very slowly. This helps him to survive while food intake is reduced drastically or stopped.

When your fatostat is set low, your body metabolism operates at a slower rate. As a result, you burn fat slowly. When your fatostat is set at a high level to maintain a low fat level, your body metabolism will operate at a higher rate, which will burn food and fat at a faster rate.

We need to learn to regulate our own fatostats—so, back to the bear for our example. His body's metabolism slows down during hibernation. This reaction is most likely the result of instinct, but it is related to the bear's physical activity slowing to an absolute minimum and food intake being reduced or stopped. In other words, when food intake and physical activity are changed, a bear's body adjusts automatically, trying to maintain whatever the new fatostat setting range is.

Are You in Hibernation?

The bear's fatostat isn't altered quickly; it shifts gradually over a year's time. In the spring, following hibernation, the bear's fatostat setting is still quite low, and its metabolism is very low. This conserves energy. Becoming more and more active, the bear consumes more food and begins to gain weight. Its fatostat now begins to slip up; its metabolism rises, compensating for the increased exercise and food intake.

Throughout the summer the bear's exercise, food intake, and weight remain pretty consistent, as does the fatostat. Then, as the fall season approaches, the bear begins to reduce its activity without decreasing the food it consumes; it may even increase food intake somewhat.

The bear's fatostat remains high for awhile, trying to maintain a relatively low fat level. But because of very little exercise and great amounts of food, the bear's fatostat slowly lowers, body metabolism slows, and a new, low fat-burning level is established.

As the bear moves into a deep hibernation period, the fatostat decreases to its lowest level. Food intake and exercise are over. The bear loses weight, but very slowly; its body is in an energy-conservation mode as a result of the fatostat's low setting.

We have all probably read about individuals who existed for years at levels of near-starvation—prisoners of war or survivors of concentration camps, for instance. Their survival, in many cases, was due to this innate metabolic setting. Bodies do adjust, but it is a slow process requiring patience and persistence.

Resetting Your Fatostat

Understanding how the fatostat works is the first step in regulating it, but the whole process of bringing a lowered fatostat up can be extremely difficult. The body resists quick change. It can be very efficient and consistent in maintaining the weight that has been established over many months and, possibly, years.

Let's say that over several years you have slowly gained twenty to thirty pounds. You want to lose it. So you cut down. You do a little exercise. After you have lost five or ten pounds, your body senses that fuel (calorie) intake has decreased and that the demands for energy have increased.

With reserve fuel (fat) decreasing, your body starts to conserve energy. It becomes determined about this energy conservation. All calories taken in are utilized very efficiently. Not a calorie goes to waste. Body metabolism is reduced to a minimum. You find it very difficult to lose much more weight. If you decrease your exercise or increase your caloric intake even slightly, you quickly gain back a pound or two or more.

Discipline is the key to success. You will need discipline to stick with your diet and exercise program—even after you reach your desired weight. If you desire to increase the rate at which your body burns calories, exercise influences your metabolism even more than diet.

Your fatostat lags behind your weight changes, resists quick changes, and is slow to establish a new balance. You must convince it by being disciplined and persistent. You must be as persistent as the bear was in setting its metabolism.

Eating Right

We have reviewed the main ingredients of permanent weight change. In summary: discipline yourself, exercise, and eat properly. Be careful to lose weight slowly and consistently, and your fatostat will be more likely to cooperate with the change.

Now let's look at how we can identify the culprits who are robbing our health and discover how to eat right.

9

Eating for the Right Reasons

A change in thinking is spreading throughout this country: People are taking more responsibility for their own health. More and more, we realize that we can change ourselves and our health. We can change our circumstances and choose our own direction. This new awareness includes our eating habits.

Before you and I can make these changes in our lives, however, we will need to change our *reasons* for eating. We will need to eat first for nutrition and fuel and second for taste and pleasure. And we will need to discover new foods and perhaps new ways to eat them.

Cutting Back on the Culprits

Before diving into a broad and varied range of new foods, you first need to be aware of foods that not only interfere with but may destroy the positive effects of good nutrition.

Reducing the consumption of sugar, salt, caffeine, protein, cholesterol, saturated fats, and highly refined and processed foods will lower the destructive demands placed on your body. It will also reduce your chances of suffering from today's common degenerative lifestyle diseases.

It is not necessary to stop eating your normal foods completely. Unless you have an immediate health problem that warrants an abrupt change, heed the wisdom of the sixth-century monk Benedict of Nursia, who advised, "Enjoy all things in moderation."

Beginning to reduce your consumption of over-processed, out-of-balance foods will be an important first step.

Sugar: The Sour Story

The typical American consumes more than one teaspoon of sugar per hour, or nearly 160 pounds per year. A twelve-ounce can of soda pop contains no less than nine teaspoons of sugar. The average American consumes 264 twelve-ounce servings per year. About 18 percent of the total calories consumed in the United States is in the form of nutrient-deficient refined sugar.

For all that sugar to be metabolized, B complex vitamins are needed. Thus sugar robs your body of important vitamins that are ordinarily used to soothe and heal the central nervous system. Refined sugar has all the nutritional co-factors removed (those vitamins and minerals that are naturally found together before processing). Because of this, the body is forced to draw on its own reserves to process sugar; this places a destructive energy demand on the body and creates distress.

British biochemist John Yudkin sees the danger:

> If only a fraction of what is already known about the effects of sugar were to be revealed in relation to any other material used as a food additive, the material would be promptly banned.

My alternative is *raw* honey in *small* amounts. Most foods already contain sugar and require no additional sweetening.

But if you must add a sweetener, raw honey is the least destructive sugar substitute. It contains several vitamins and minerals not found in refined sugar—Vitamin A; several vitamins from the B complex family; and vital enzymes, hormones, and minerals, such as phosphorus, potassium, calcium, sodium, sulphur, iron, magnesium, and manganese. I don't want to mislead you; they come in very modest amounts, but they are in perfect balance and do have some nutritive value.

Since early recorded history, raw honey has been used for its medicinal and nutritional qualities. Most centenarians in Bulgaria and Russia consistently use raw honey in their diets.

Hooked on Sugar

We've only begun to understand the effects and the danger of our excessive intake of sugar. Take the story of Bob Staeheli. He knew he had a problem but couldn't put his finger on exactly what it was. When his daughter married, he would have given anything to look sharp in his white tuxedo.

Bob was overweight. That was obvious. But the problem seemed deeper than the excess poundage that hung over his overstrained belt. He didn't feel right stuffed into that tux, and he decided to do something about it.

Bob Staeheli didn't take the usual route of dieting and exercise. Instead, he checked himself into a chemical dependency treatment center. His problem was neither alcohol nor drugs. His problem was sugar. Bob was hooked on it.

"We don't regard sugar as a chemical, but many scientists and writers today are saying it is as much of a drug as heroin," says Staeheli.

The story behind the story is hypoglycemia and the effects sugar has on the body. According to Staeheli, his sugar metabolism caused nervousness, irritability, depression, fatigue, and aggressive behavior, among other things.

Sugar and Alcoholism

These same symptoms are common among alcoholics. Staeheli says that at the treatment center he learned that "Ninety to ninety-five percent of all alcoholics are suffering from hypoglycemia—low blood sugar." Because alcohol is the most concentrated sugar known to man, an alcoholic can get relief from his symptoms within seconds of a swallow of liquor. When his blood sugar drops, the alcoholic has to go to the bar. In Bob Staeheli's case, it was to the local pie shop.

Once the abused substance is removed from an alcoholic—or an individual hooked on sugar—he often continues to suffer from the nervousness and depression previously experienced; his body's metabolism and natural chemical balance has been thrown out of kilter after years of heavy doses of sugar, alcohol, and refined sugar.

These symptoms can be treated with a natural diet and with a thorough knowledge of the body's physiology. It was an uphill battle, but Bob Staeheli's life has changed dramatically due to his reduction of sugar.

Please Don't Pass the Salt

We have already briefly discussed the American misuse of salt. Americans today consume an average of ten pounds of salt per person annually, most of which is contained in processed foods. That's *ten times* more than we need!

We require only about 200 milligrams of salt per day. As salt-happy Americans, our individual intake can range from six to forty times that amount. Approximately two of those ten pounds are added at home.

No wonder. Our taste for the substance starts early. Baby food manufacturers often add it to their products. Babies, of course, have no innate taste for salt, but their parents buy the salty-tasting foods because they taste good to themselves.

Promoters are smart enough to add salt to the food for this reason.

Our family went out for breakfast one Sunday morning after church. While waiting for our food, I observed a couple and their two children at a nearby table. The children were about three to five years old. Before the children even had a chance to taste their food, their father thoroughly salted it.

Once a taste has been "learned" or acquired, it is a difficult addiction to give up, so babies who learn to love salt become salt-lovers as adults. The fact that many processed and packaged foods are saturated with salt before we purchase them makes this a doubly difficult addiction, requiring great effort to give up. Even when we *choose* to cut down, it's a battle.

You'll Never Miss It

Salt decreases the ability of vitamins to build and rebuild nerve tissues. It also forces potassium out of the body, which changes the delicate, acid-alkaline balance of the nerve tissue cells. This could mean a critically-tense and restricted nervous system. It raises the nerve tissue's sensitivity and irritability. In this state, the nervous system simply is not able to handle demands. There also seems to be a strong relationship between salt consumption and high blood pressure.

Your new, low-sodium or salt-free diet doesn't have to be bland or tasteless. Converts to the low-sodium lifestyle find, to their surprise, that when salt is reduced or removed completely, taste buds gradually begin tasting the food again instead of just the salt. Don't let anyone tell you that a healthy lifestyle is boring, painful, or flavorless. You'll see what I mean when you begin to use spices, herbs, and other natural flavorings instead of salt.

The American Heart Association publishes a very good 145-page book, *Cooking Without Your Salt Shaker.*

You can purchase one from your closest Heart Association affiliate.

Cutting Down on Caffeine

Caffeine is found in coffee, tea, cola, and chocolate. Contrary to what most people believe, caffeine is a drug. Taken in excess, it can cause stomach acid secretions leading to heartburn and bleeding ulcers. And I don't have to tell you what several cups of coffee can do to your nervous system.

Caffeine has been linked to increased heart rate and blood pressure, restlessness, and disturbed sleep. Birth defects, diabetes, kidney failure, and cancer of the pancreas are also on caffeine's hit list.

One or two cups each day are okay for most people, providing they aren't getting caffeine from any other source. Although moderation may be acceptable, abstinence is best.

The Truth About Saturated Fats

Fat consumption currently accounts for about 42 percent of the average American diet. You can see my cause for concern when I inform you that *10 percent* is ideal. High consumption of saturated fats is associated with dangerous blood cholesterol levels, which is a risk factor for stroke and heart disease.

Animal foods, especially red meats, are high in saturated fats. The average American consumes about 167 pounds per year. Research has shown that by reducing the number of animal foods eaten and replacing them with high fiber vegetables, grains, and fruits, you will likely have a healthier blood cholesterol level and reduce your risks.

The Danger of Hydrogenated Fats

Hydrogenated fats are created when natural polyunsaturated fat, derived from plants, is heated and then saturated with hydrogen. This process retards spoilage, but it also destroys the essential fatty acids. Our cells don't know what to do with this fragmented, unnatural fat. The body cannot assimilate them. If and when it is unable to eliminate these fats, the body may deposit them in the body someplace in the circulatory system.

Joe D. Nichols, M.D., in his book, *Please, Doctor, Do Something,* calls hydrogenated fats "the number one cause of heart disease today."

Read labels. Do your best to avoid hydrogenated fats in such products as margarine, shortening, peanut butter, bakery products, crackers, and breads.

Now check your cupboard. Is it filled with oils that will not spoil when stored at room temperature? Oils without hydrogenated fats need to be refrigerated. Purchase only *cold pressed* oil. This is a process used to extract the oil from its vegetable source. The label will say "cold pressed." Health food stores carry this type of oil. Keep it refrigerated, and use it before it spoils.

What is Serum Cholesterol?

We hear a lot about cholesterol these days and the danger it presents to our health, but few people understand what it really is. Serum cholesterol is a measure of the total amount of cholesterol in the blood. Your body makes and needs cholesterol, but as the blood level elevates problems arise.

Serum cholesterol consists of basically two types of cholesterol:

HDL (high density lipoprotein), which accounts for about 20 percent of the total, acts like a garbage truck as it passes through the blood stream. It picks up the excess cholesterol and carries it to the liver where it is broken down and eliminated.

LDL (low density lipoprotein), which accounts for the balance of the cholesterol in the blood, can be harmful in excess and has a tendency to attach itself to the walls of the arteries and eventually reduce blood flow or clog arteries.

Checking Your Cholesterol

To get a measurement of your cholesterol levels, you previously needed to make an appointment with your doctor. After fasting for eight hours, your blood samples would be taken and analyzed by a medical laboratory. You may have had to wait two weeks for results. The cost of measuring your cholesterol levels probably ranged between twenty and sixty dollars.

The technological advantages of portable cholesterol analyzers puts mass public screenings at your fingertips. Blood cholesterol can now be measured from a fingerstick sample of blood, the results can be obtained in three to five minutes, and the cost is usually less than ten dollars. Watch for opportunities in your community where these mass screenings are available.

Less than 10 percent of the American adult population know what their cholesterol levels are. I am convinced knowing your cholesterol level is at least as important as knowing your blood pressure. The following guidelines will help you understand your blood cholesterol readings.

Blood Cholesterol Levels

Age	Recommended	ModerateRisk	High Risk
20-29	under 180mg/dL	200-220mg/dL	220+mg/dL
30-39	under 200mg/dL	220-240mg/dL	240+mg/dL
40+	under 200mg/dL	240-260mg/dL	260+mg/dL

Because there are no obvious symptoms of high blood cholesterol, make sure you have it checked again within three years even if your current level is in the normal range.

Cholesterol levels range anywhere from 150-350 milligrams. While 220 milligrams is considered normal for adults, this level varies with age, race, and sex. A serum cholesterol level of 250 milligrams and above increases your risk of a heart attack or stoke three times greater than when it is 190 or less.

Whenever your cholesterol level is in the moderate or high risk range, you should begin working with your health professional to reduce it through exercise and diet. Certain lifestyle factors negatively affect cholesterol levels. These include smoking, obesity, fast-forward behavior, and some oral contraceptives.

Diet definitely affects cholesterol levels. The average American consumes twice as much cholesterol than is considered healthy. Some of the common foods high in cholesterol are:

- Whole milk
- Butter
- Eggs
- Cheese
- Liver
- Beef
- Pork
- Lamb
- Dark fowl
- Shrimp
- Lobster
- Tuna fish (packed in oil)

Some foods positively influence cholesterol levels and can actually lower your numbers. We should probably add or increase the prevalence of these foods in our diets. Certain high-fiber foods like carrots, broccoli, and oats lower cholesterol. Pectin, which is found in fresh fruit, also contributes to cleansing our systems of these dangerous fats.

Preparing foods with oils that are high in polyunsaturated fats is best. Switch to corn, safflower, sesame, soybean, and

sunflower oils. Olive oil, a monounsaturated fat, is also helpful. Consuming fish and fish oil, which contain omega-3 fatty
acids, also contributes to healthy cholesterol levels.

Too Much Protein

My next suggestion is that you reduce the gross overconsumption of protein. We have been taught that proteins are
the building blocks to our health, and they actually were—
while we were growing. But now, as adults, the house is
already built. We need only enough protein to take care of
maintenance.

Excess protein cannot be stored. Overconsumption taxes
the kidneys and the entire metabolic system. In a recent study
performed by the Harvard Medical School, researchers
emphasized a clear link between high protein consumption
and kidney disease.

Americans consume 150 to 200 grams of protein a day,
and that is two to three times the necessary amount.
The National Research Council recommends .42 grams of
protein daily per pound of body weight. A person weighing 200 pounds would need eighty-four grams. Generally,
thirty to fifty grams is about right for the average individual.
Seventy grams is high even for pregnant women and people experiencing high levels of physical and psychological
stress.

Another myth is that animal products are our best source
of protein—the only source of complete protein. Actually,
animal protein is not superior to protein derived from
vegetable sources. Contrary to common belief, complete or
nearly complete protein can be found in the following foods:

- almonds
- peanuts
- sunflower seeds
- sesame seeds

- soybeans
- millet
- buckwheat
- all sprouted seeds
- leafy green vegetables
- potatoes

Refined Flour—Dressed to Kill

You already know that highly refined and processed foods are destructive due to the substances *added to* them (fat, sugar, salt). But they are also hard on the body because of the ingredients *missing* from them. Processed foods are lower in nutritional value and fiber than natural and raw foods.

Refined white flour contains far less bran, protein, calcium, phosphorous, iron, thiamine, riboflavin, niacin, and potassium than whole wheat flour. Since 18 percent of the average American diet consists of nutrient-deficient processed white flour, it would be wonderful if all that flour could be replaced with whole grain flours.

Accomplishing this is quite difficult because emotions as well as physical hunger are involved. A succulent berry pie or a thick slice of cake can entice us because we know how good they will taste. Subconsciously we are also filling an emotional need.

Our emotional needs should be tempered by such rational questions as:

What do I want to accomplish today?
What kind of fuel can a piece of pie provide?
What damage can chocolate cake do to my body?

When we question ourselves this way, we may be more inclined to reach for food that will provide us with good taste *and* the energy we really need.

How to Eat Right

You have just read about a number of ways we can improve our diets and become more nutritionally fit. Let's summarize these concepts. The following list of nutritional action alternatives is based primarily on a set of dietary goals released by the Senate Select Committee on Nutrition and Human Needs and "Life Extending Tips" published by the American Longevity Association.

1. *Keep energy intake equal to energy expenditure.* Do not take in more fuel than you will use. By keeping caloric intake and weight low, you will also help slow the aging process.

2. *Reduce consumption of highly refined and processed foods.* There is much less nutrition and bran in processed food than in raw food. Experts speculate that the highly refined and processed diet is a major risk factor in cancer of the colon and rectum. They also believe that this "industrialized diet" is a major risk factor in many of the degenerative diseases of our society.

3. *Reduce consumption of all refined and processed sugars.* The average American consumes approximately 160 pounds of sugar a year. In the early 1900s, it was approximately five pounds. Sugar has been shown to reduce the white blood cells' ability to resist germs; in other words, sugar undermines the front-line defense of your immune system. Sugar has also been shown to reduce Vitamin C levels, which is highly important for optimum effectiveness of the immune system.

4. *Reduce consumption of sodium chloride (salt).* Unrefined sea salt without anti-caking agents is better than refined table salt (100 percent sodium chloride) because of its technical make-up—75 percent sodium chloride and 25 percent balanced trace elements and minerals such as magnesium and calcium. Although sea salt can also be harmful

in large quantities, it is certainly better than pure sodium chloride. Vegetable salt is another, safer alternative.

5. *Reduce consumption of caffeine.* Moderation is the key. Limit your daily intake of caffeine to two or three cups of coffee, maximum.

6. *Reduce consumption of saturated fats.* Saturated fats are commonly found in animal meats and dairy products. Replace this diet with proteins found in vegetable products, fish, and poultry. A low fat diet helps prevent heart disease and cancer.

7. *Reduce consumption of hydrogenated fats.* When foods are hydrogenated, fatty acids are altered so they can no longer be metabolized properly by the cells. Trying to metabolize hydrogenated fats is like trying to put a house key into the car ignition—it just doesn't fit.

8. *Reduce consumption of foods high in cholesterol.* Foods containing high levels of cholesterol include animal meats, dairy products, shrimp, lobster, and tuna fish packed in oil. We consume two to three times more cholesterol than we need, which contributes to the risk of heart disease and stroke. Substitute vegetables often; they have actually been shown to lower blood cholesterol. Cholesterol-lowering oil has also been found in herring, salmon, sardines, anchovies, and mackerel.

9. *Reduce the consumption of protein.* The Hunzakuts, who are virtually free of westernized diseases such as heart disease, cancer, diabetes, and arthritis, consume only about thirty grams of protein per day. Other people who enjoy long life spans—including the Yucatan Indians, the Bulgarians, the Abkhasians, and the Vilcabambas—also have low protein diets.

10. *Breathe clean, fresh air.* This rule may seem out of place in a nutritional discussion, but the quantity and quality of the air we breathe is essential to the maintenance of healthful lives. Breathe slowly and deeply. The effectiveness of our delivery system—the cardiovascular and respiratory

systems—is a key to making oxygen available to the body on a cellular level.

11. *Increase consumption of raw foods.* There is more nutrition and fiber in raw food such as vegetables, fruits, whole grains, seeds, and nuts than in the processed foods we are accustomed to eating. The raw seed and nut family contain exceptional amounts of protein, fiber, polyunsaturated fats, and virtually the entire chart of vitamins and minerals. Most varieties of seeds and nuts are good for you, but some are better than others. When overall nutritional value and calories are compared, the winners are: raw almonds, peanuts, pumpkin seeds, sunflower seeds, and sesame seeds. The runners up include: brazil nuts, walnuts, roasted almonds, roasted peanuts, filberts, and pistachios. In short, the closer we stay to the natural food chain, the healthier we will be.

12. *Increase consumption of clean hard water.* Drink six to ten glasses per day *between meals*. Worldwide research continues to show that when people drink naturally mineralized hard water rather than soft water they enjoy better health, less tooth decay, less heart disease, less diabetes, and less mineral deficiency diseases (such as osteoporosis) than people who don't drink hard water. For regular daily use, clean well or spring water is best. Use a good water cleansing or filtering system that will eliminate chlorine and other cancer-causing chemicals yet still provide you with essential minerals.

Keep it Simple

Eating for the right reasons and in the right ways takes practice. So don't panic. Look over this list and begin to make changes at the point that will benefit your health but not cause you to become discouraged.

You may want to start by purchasing a water filtering system and keeping a bottle of cold water in the refrigerator.

Replace whole milk with 2 percent and then move on to skim milk. If you throw out the salt box and buy sea salt instead, your family probably won't even notice.

With a little thought and imagination, you can probably think of many ways to improve your eating habits without feeling like you're depriving yourself. Before you know it, you'll be eating healthier, feeling better, and inspired to new levels of discipline in other areas of your life.

10
The Best Diet in the World

Mrs. Leonard, a 107-year-old New Zealander, is often asked the secret of her longevity. She says, it's not the hand-rolled cigarettes she smokes, nor the pipe, which she has enjoyed since she was five. No, the secret of her 107 years is that every day she is careful to eat lots and lots of candy.

There are rare exceptions to the lifestyles we now know produce healthy and productive lives. Many factors could account for Mrs. Leonard's impressive age, including how much she smoked, whether or not she inhaled, her diet, whether she exercised, and, of course, genetics. People love to hear stories like hers because to them it seems proof that it doesn't matter how we live.

If you're willing to wager—in the giant lottery of life—that you are one of the world's rare exceptions, I have a gold mine in North Dakota I'd like to talk to you about. My hopes are still pinned on the active pursuit of wellness—which brings us to the next step in aggressively creating a lifestyle you can live with: *nutrition and its by-products—energy and toxins.*

Pure and Simple

In my research, I have come across four present-day civilizations whose diets remain very close to the natural food chain. These individuals seem to have little difficulty living to ninety, one hundred, and beyond while still possessing the physical capabilities of a forty or fifty-year-old American.

Please keep in mind, they know absolutely nothing about calories, carbohydrates, vitamins, and minerals. Their simple, health-promoting diets consist of natural, unrefined, unsweetened, and unprocessed foods grown in healthy, chemical-free, organic soil.

Although these four civilizations live in completely different areas of the world and their diets do vary slightly, they have one thing in common. Their diets consist mainly of food from plants. Almost invariably they are vegetarians.

There are actually four different levels of vegetarianism:

1. The vegan
2. The lactovegetarian
3. The ovolactovegetarian
4. The semi-vegetarian

The *vegan's* diet is composed exclusively of plant foods without any animal products. Certain vegans won't even wear animal products.

The *lactovegetarian's* diet is similar to the vegan's, but she or he also consumes dairy products.

The *ovolactovegetarian* adds eggs and dairy products to the basic foundation of plant foods.

The last and largest group of vegetarians is called *semi-vegetarian*. For the past twelve years I have been part of this group. We supplement our basic diet of plant foods with dairy products, eggs, fish, poultry, and, occasionally, lean red meat.

The Optimal Diet

A healthy diet, as we have seen in several modern civilizations where people live robust lives past one hundred years, is:

1. Low in protein, red meat, and saturated fats.
2. High in fiber, seeds, nuts, grains, beans, and fresh vegetables and fruits.

This is an optimal diet for two reasons. First, these foods come from natural sources. They are rich in nutrients. That means your body can easily convert them to energy. The second reason these foods are part of the optimal diet is because of their fiber content, which helps regulate the rate at which nutrients are metabolized. The fiber also helps to transport toxins and wastes from the body.

I came to the decision to join the ranks of the semi-vegetarian when I realized how much healthier vegetarian foods were—and when I discovered that the diet is at least as tasteful as my heavy meat diet was. As you may have gathered, I was brought up on the typical midwestern meat and potatoes meals.

Who Needs Meat?

The modern westernized diet of too many animal products, especially red meat, provides us with an excess of protein and saturated fats. The effects of this sort of eating are devastating.

A study published in the *Journal of the American Medical Association* reported that the blood pressure of people whose diet was based on meat was higher than those eating semi-vegetarian diets. The vegetarians as a group were also leaner than their meat-eating counterparts, and they didn't consciously diet.

There has also been clear proof that vegetarianism is the better diet for human beings based on our biological make-up. Unlike the carnivorous animals—dogs, lions, tigers—we lack the important enzyme, *uricase,* that renders a toxic meat by-product called uric acid harmless. Anatomically, the carnivore has a short intestinal canal, ideal for meat digestion. Ours is long. Meat putrefies during the digestive cycle and forms "natural gas."

Most people balk when I suggest they try a semi-vegetarian diet. They fear that by giving up steak, hamburgers, and ham sandwiches, they will be sacrificing the pleasures of eating. If it's good for me, they reason, it won't taste good. But as Mikey discovered in the classic TV cereal commercial, even good food can taste good.

Give it Time

Too often we resist change because we don't have enough facts. Let me assure you, vegetarian and semi-vegetarian diets need not be boring or bland. There are a number of exotic and nutritional recipes waiting to be tried.

It may take time for you to become accustomed to the new foods and methods of preparation, but nearly all people who are willing to try vegetarian eating discover that they can be seduced by the large variety of mouth-watering and nutritious dishes available. Vegetarianism, I have found, is an exceptionally worthwhile adventure.

Your tastes will change. To your own amazement, you'll find that when you want to eat for taste or pleasure, you will most often reach for something that tastes great and is good for you as well. That's the pleasure of vegetarian eating. Virtually every food in your diet is nutritionally beneficial.

One word of caution: start slowly. As with an exercise program, your body needs to adjust to the change—the new demands placed upon it. This takes time and should be accomplished gradually.

Eating well is not a trend or a fad. Various forms of vegetarianism have been practiced throughout history. Join me and a host of famous people who practiced vegetarian eating habits: Leonardo da Vinci, George Bernard Shaw, Henry David Thoreau, Leo Tolstoy—I could go on and on. But I guarantee your efforts to join this distinguished group will be rewarded. This chapter contains a list of vegetarian cookbooks that will help you get started.

How to Make it Taste Good

Now comes the hard part—having something better waiting in the wings after you've denied yourself a sundae.

Whatever food it is, it needs to appeal at least as strongly to the eye and the palate as the delectable morsel you've just passed up. People will rarely sacrifice a pleasurable pastime like eating unless they have something else to take its place.

If your new nutritional program is to succeed, you must provide yourself natural, healthy foods that can also fill your emotional needs for taste and pleasure. This may be a real battle at first, but, with practice, it will become progressively easier.

Your new diet can consist of a variety of:

- Grains
- Seeds
- Nuts
- Beans
- Fresh vegetables
- Fresh fruits

You may choose to supplement this basic vegetarian diet with:

- Low-fat dairy products
- Fish

- Skinless poultry
- Lean red meat (occasionally)

From these ingredients you can make hundreds of delicious, good-looking, exotic, and otherwise delightful meals. Try recipes in vegetarian cookbooks. I can recommend:

Marilyn Diamond's *The Common Sense Guide to a New Way of Eating*. Santa Monica, CA: Golden Glow Publishers.
The New American Vegetarian Menu Cookbook. Emmaus, PA: Rodale Books.
Rodale's Basic Natural Foods Cookbook. Emmaus, PA: Rodale Books.
Feasting on Raw Foods, Charles Gerras, Ed. Emmaus, PA: Rodale Books.
Marti Wheeler's *116 Tantalizing Good-Health Recipes*. Ft. Pierce, FL: Life Science.
Homemaker's Guide to Foods for Pleasure & Health. Tampa, FL: Natural Hygiene Press.
Norman Shealy's *Speedy Gourmet*. Fair Grove, MI: Brindabella Books.

Learning How to Eat

When you begin to eat high energy foods as fuel, you'll want to watch the amount you eat. It's important to avoid taking in more fuel than your body can use and efficiently store; overeating can be toxic.

1. *Your energy intake should be equal to energy expenditure.* For example, 75 percent of your calories should be consumed before evening because during the day your body needs the most energy. I usually consume 25 percent of my daily calories at breakfast and 50 percent at lunch (since I need most of my energy in the afternoon). In the evening, my activities have slowed. I avoid going to bed with a full

stomach because I've found that this tendency really does promote excess pounds. Caloric intake should coincide with the body's needs.

2. *Stop eating before you feel full.* This is a tough habit to break. Overeating is easy to do, so it's healthy to get into the habit of slightly undereating.

3. *Eat slowly.* It takes the brain about twenty minutes to register that the stomach is content. Fast eaters often consume twice as much as their bodies need or want; their brains don't relay the "stomach full" message until it's too late. Remember, appetites grow by habitual overeating.

4. *Eat smaller meals more often.* Your body actually handles smaller quantities of food more efficiently. Eating four to five light meals will fuel the body more efficiently than three heavy ones.

Vitamin Supplements and the American Diet

People who are becoming more conscious of nutrition frequently ask me, "Are food supplements necessary?" Let me give you some information that will help you decide for yourself.

Ideally, all essential vitamins, minerals, and nutrients should be obtained through our diets. Unfortunately, much of the nutrients are gone from our food by the time we eat it. The first culprits to diminish our food's nutritional value (while it is still in the ground!) are the lack of naturally fertile soil and the addition of chemical fertilizers.

Once harvested, our food is further altered to "improve" its flavor or appearance. After being colored, flavored, fumigated, preserved, texturized, bleached, and so on, food can lose much of its nutritional value. Once we get these foods home, they continue to lose nutritional value until we finally eat them.

Cooking further robs them of nutritive value. When our diets are based on cooked food—in which many of the enzymes are destroyed and the nutrients impaired—we're in trouble, dietetically. The cooked food diet, with its great scarcity of fiber, has repeatedly been shown to result in constipation, diverticulosis, colitis, and other digestive problems. Arthritis and many other degenerative ailments are considered by some scientists and hygienists to be diseases of this form of eating.

It's possible that as much as 98 percent of our food's nutrients may be lost before we eat it, not to mention its lack of fiber. Obviously, we may have great difficulty fulfilling our nutritional and fiber needs solely from the foods we eat— especially when we cook them to the extent we are accustomed.

Although I consider my diet a healthy one, I supplement it with vitamins, minerals, and fiber, as insurance. This practice helps me prevent deficiencies, illness, and disease.

You Can't Improve on Nature

"On the whole," says Dr. A. J. Carlson of Chicago University, "we can trust the wisdom of nature further than the chemist." Experience and history tell us that we cannot fool our bodies with fragmented foods, man-made drugs, and artificial sweeteners. Each time we try, our sandwich lands jelly-side down.

A ten-year study in America involved 900 cats who were fed processed foods. The cats developed multiple degenerative diseases and became extinct by the third generation. Cats that were fed raw, natural foods were consistently healthy generation after generation, producing large, healthy litters.

Stay close to the natural food chain, and you will find it easier to achieve and maintain nutritional balance. When you eat overprocessed and chemical-laced food, your body has a difficult time producing the energy necessary to sustain and propel you—especially if you are highly active or pregnant.

Your body feels the effects of fresh, natural food; it's almost like finding the mother lode in a gold mine. It's rich, easy-to-process, and there's little waste. What an excellent return!

Conversely, eating highly-processed and chemical-laden food is something like tiny veins of gold. The gold's there somewhere, but only sparsely. It's difficult to process, there's much waste, and the return is poor.

Natural or Synthetic Vitamins?

You have a choice—natural vitamins or synthetic vitamins made by man. They may look the same in the laboratory, but the unknown ingredients in vitamins found in their natural state provide the key that unlocks the door to the body's metabolism.

Natural living foods, with their live vitamins and organic minerals all in natural balance as a result of the sun, water, soils, minerals, and living bacteria, are a better foundation for our biological needs than dead, inert materials. Numerous studies show that natural vitamins have greater health benefits than processed and synthetic supplements.

In Sweden, silver foxes who were fed natural vitamins grew normally, developed beautiful fur, and enjoyed excellent health. The group fed the same amount of synthetic B-vitamins failed to grow normally, had inferior fur, and contracted numerous diseases. Only living matter has the power to *act;* only living matter can recreate itself.

Therefore, I don't recommend synthetic vitamins—with one exception: when synthetic vitamins are used for therapeutic purposes. For example, large doses of ascorbic acid, a synthetic vitamin C, have been used successfully in acute cases of poisoning and infections. Norman Cousins used the method along with his celebrated humor therapy to overcome a degenerative disease of the spinal column.

In large doses, synthetic vitamins are much like drugs. They are fast-acting and at select times can be used to treat ill health. But, like drugs, treatment should be short-term, under medical supervision, and only when necessary.

I recommend natural vitamins for use as supplements to a vegetarian or semi-vegetarian diet. It is this combination that I believe will deliver optimal nutritional health and provide the foundation for the energy and vitality you desire.

When you choose your mineral supplementation, be aware that the terms organic, inorganic, natural, and synthetic have little meaning. All minerals originate in mother earth. The main concern is how easily they are absorbed, assimilated, or utilized by the body rather than where they come from.

How to Get What You Need

No multiple supplement formulation is perfect. Each has its strong and weak points. Whatever your individual needs are, find the one closest to those needs, and then add other supplements accordingly.

The best time to take vitamins and supplements is with or shortly after your meals. They are assimilated better at that time. The exceptions to this rule of thumb are normally indicated in the directions for use.

It's also best to divide your supplements into portions so you take some with each meal rather than taking them all at once. Most multiple supplements will require that you take two to four tablets per day to reach the potency listed on the container. For example, suppose that three tablets per day of your supplement supplied calcium 300 mg., magnesium 150 mg., Vitamin D 400 IU. If this were the case, you would take one tablet at each meal. The body has a tendency to throw off most excesses, so taking them gradually assists the body in its absorption.

When deciding *where* to buy supplements, I recommend health food stores or independent distributors instead of drug stores. The latter normally stocks synthetic supplements. There are exceptions to this rule, but you'll need to shop around.

Base your decision to buy one supplement over another on product quality versus cost. I would not say that the highest priced supplement is necessarily best, but keep in mind that it costs suppliers more to produce quality supplements. Begin gathering information ahead of time, and choose carefully, with a thorough knowledge and trust of the product.

Slow and Simple

Remember the long-lived people we talked about previously, and be encouraged. Through common sense, they eat simple, fresh, and unrefined whole foods. Although they know nothing about calories, vitamins, and minerals, their diets contain a complex balance of nutrients that provide all the elements their bodies need—the way God planned.

You can learn to eat this way. But like anything else—practice makes perfect. Once again, my advice is to start simple. Make changes slowly and don't try to change your diet all at once.

When there are other family members to consider, you may be met with some resistance. But the more you know about why you are eating certain foods and not others, the easier it will be to persuade them to change.

Change is never easy. But being sick and tired isn't any fun either. Most adults—and even children—will respond positively to eating right when they understand the results they can expect.

11

Use It or Lose It!

I am convinced that one of the primary causes of disease is an inefficient elimination system that allows toxins to accumulate in the body. These toxins block the assimilation of nutrients into the cells, put a drain on the body's energy reservoir, and undermine the body's own innate healing capabilities.

Eliminating toxins and waste products from our body cells is rarely talked about. Yet, it is essential—even critical—to overall energy and health. We need to cleanse our body tissues thoroughly of foreign substances and the natural waste by-products of normal body metabolism.

Even if our cells receive the proper amount of oxygen and nutrition, they cannot assimilate nutrients when they are surrounded by toxins, poisons, and waste products; they become "toxic waste sites." We are only as healthy as our cells.

If we increase the efficiency of our internal cleansing systems, we improve our health, our level of energy, and our ability to be consistently productive. Therefore, "If you can't use it, lose it!"

The Immortal Living Cell?

French scientist Dr. Alexis Carrell, at the Rockefeller Institute of Medical Research, set out to demonstrate that a cell could live indefinitely under optimum conditions. He placed the heart tissue cells of a chicken embryo into an incubator. The heart tissue rested in a nourishing plasma solution, which was changed every day to remove wastes excreted by the heart tissue.

The tissue remained alive for thirty-four years—that's *eight times* longer than the average chicken lives! It died only when an assistant forgot to change the plasma fluid. The cells, immersed in toxic substances produced by their own metabolism, were unable to survive.

Dr. Carrell concluded,

> The cell is immortal. It is merely the fluid in which it floats that degenerates. Renew this fluid at intervals, give the cell something upon which to feed, and so far as we know, the pulsation of life may go on forever.

Ridding the body of toxins is a major step toward healthy cells and a healthy body. Without proper internal cleansing, our bodies will have trouble assimilating vitamins and minerals. We can be eating the most nutritious foods and taking the finest supplements yet still suffer nutritional deficiencies.

Are You Poisoning Yourself?

Toxemia is an illness caused by toxins in the bloodstream, which can become poisoned in two ways. One is from without—air we breathe, water we drink, food we eat, and drugs we take. The other is from within as a result of normal bodily functions and is called *autointoxication*.

Let's look at an example that may help you understand how autointoxication occurs. You are probably familiar with the general function of an automobile engine. You put fuel into the gas tank, which is fed into the carburetor where it is mixed with air. This fuel and air mixture is then drawn into the motor, where it is ignited by the spark plugs. The internal combustion produces the energy that enables the car to run.

Waste products are produced as a result of this internal combustion, and they must be eliminated from the motor. The primary poisonous substance is carbon monoxide, which is forced out the tail pipe. In addition, there are waste products produced inside the engine as a result of wear and tear. The greater the demands placed on the motor, the greater the wear and tear, and the greater the amount of waste by-products.

These by-products are absorbed primarily by the oil that circulates within the motor. As the oil circulates through the oil filter, some of the by-products are filtered out; some settle to the bottom of the motor's oil pan; and some remain in the oil.

Most engines will give us trouble-free service if the exhaust system doesn't become clogged and if the oil and filter are changed regularly. With rare exceptions, motors kept clean by consistently eliminating waste by-products will last for a long, long time. When waste products are not eliminated regularly, they will cause unnecessary wear and tear and, probably, premature breakdown.

Energy Conversion

Consider the similarities between the function of an automobile engine and your body. You take food and water into your body, where it is processed through your digestive system into usable fuel. The usable nutrients are then combined with oxygen and enzymes, which are located primarily within the muscle mass. The resulting catalytic action provides the energy you need to function.

Like the car engine, your body reacts to the greater demands placed on it by producing greater amounts of by-products that must be eliminated.

To complete the analogy, we exhale carbon dioxide. The lymphatic and circulatory systems work like the car's oil system to transport the remaining internal waste to the liver and kidneys, which serve as the main filters.

The process of eliminating toxins, poisons, and waste products from our systems is as important as putting quality fuel in. Our energy levels, vitality, health, and longevity depend upon how well we do both. The skin, bladder, and colon are the main parts of our bodies that eliminate toxins and wastes. We need to understand each.

Your Skin—the Third Kidney

The skin is our largest and most overlooked cleansing organ. It is estimated that one third of all body wastes are eliminated through the skin. Hundreds of thousands of sweat glands gather impurities and excrete them. Whenever we perspire, we cleanse wastes from our systems. No wonder the skin has been called our "third kidney."

The chemical composition of sweat is similar to urine, and more than one pound of these wastes are expelled through and evaporate off the skin each day. The skin also absorbs vital oxygen, minerals, and nutrients. Therefore, keeping the channels in the skin open is vital to natural body balance and health.

How do we help this occur?

1. Wearing clothes of natural fibers—clothes that "breathe"—will enhance this healthy exchange.

2. Exercise, steam rooms, and saunas complement the skin's natural function because they stimulate the pores to expel impurities via sweating.

3. Regular bathing also helps—when done correctly. While bathing, use a mild ph-balanced soap—but only on oily areas. A wet washcloth or loofah sponge alone is enough for cleaning the rest of your skin. Many commercial soaps clog pores, some will dry the skin, and some will do both. Choose your soap carefully, and then use it only sparingly.

The Dry Brush Skin Massage

Few people know of and even fewer utilize the dry brush skin massage, but it is a powerful tool that can increase the skin's effectiveness.

It has a number of health benefits: It feels good; removes dead layers of skin, toxins, and impurities; and helps keep pores open so they can feed and cleanse the body with greater capacity. The nerve endings in the skin are stimulated, and circulation in underlying tissues, organs, and blood vessels is revitalized.

Besides improving your health and your skin's efficiency as an elimination organ, the dry brush massage can help prevent premature aging. It definitely improves how you feel and how you look.

Although it doesn't contribute to aerobic fitness, the dry brush skin massage is as invigorating as twenty minutes of aerobic exercise. You can purchase this wonderful natural fiber brush at most health food stores.

Flushing Out the Bladder and Kidneys

The bladder and kidneys filter toxic wastes from about 1700 gallons of blood that pass through them daily. The concentration of these toxins are determined by air, water, food, and drug consumption as well as by how well the body is eliminating waste by-products.

When you are under physical or emotional strain, your body metabolism steps up to accommodate the demand.

As a result, additional waste by-products are produced. When you exercise or face a stressful event, you need more water. When your system is waging an all-out war on the flu, a cold, etc., these demands (stress) occur throughout your body. There are millions and millions of dead cells left after the fight. Water helps flush them out of your body, but it will require more than usual.

How do You Spell Relief?

Urine is an accurate indicator of the body's current need for water; its color is the key. When urine is darker than a light yellow, the concentration of toxins is too high and the body needs more unpolluted water.

Your body is 70 percent liquid, so six to ten glasses of water a day really are *crucial* for your body and urinary system to function properly. Water replaces fluids lost to sweat, tearing eyes, running noses, and diarrhea. They help fight sore throats, allergies, fever, infection, constipation, and colds.

Water is a natural remedy for many common ills. How do you spell relief? W-A-T-E-R. As I mentioned earlier, your best choice is filtered, naturally mineralized water.

To help you fully appreciate its importance, think of your body as a steam engine. It needs both fuel and fire to run; but without water, it can't produce energy. It will overheat and could very well self-destruct. The body needs water; without it, the body cannot produce energy.

I've met thousands of people over the years as I have conducted seminars and workshops, but rarely have I come across someone who drinks enough water. At work, keep a glass of cool water at your desk or work station to sip on at all times. A slice or two of lemon or lime adds a pleasant, mild taste that entices the taste buds.

Once you begin consuming sufficient water, you'll be absolutely amazed at how much better you feel and how much more energy you have. Try it!

Your Colon—A Toxic Waste Site?

The largest mass of wastes is eliminated through the colon. When you eat, your food passes through the digestive system, where your body then absorbs what nutrients it can use.

The elements that cannot be assimilated are waste substances that collect in the colon. When the body's disposal system is not functioning effectively, the level of toxicity in the body begins to rise. When that happens, we drastically increase our risk of cellular destruction.

An underactive colon allows wastes to stay in our systems, decaying and producing poisons that will pollute our entire bodies. This clearly creates distress, a destructive demand placed on the body, and subsequently causes a subtle drain on the energy reservoir.

Inefficient colons also prevent our bodies from taking in the vitamins and minerals they need. You could be eating the healthiest, most nutritional foods available and be religiously taking an adequate supply of supplements yet still suffer nutritional deficiencies.

Dead Before Fifty?

In 1978, Anthony Sattilaro, M.D., Chief Operating Officer of Methodist Hospital in Philadelphia, was stricken with prostatic cancer at age forty-seven. Following surgery and other traditional treatments, he was told he might not see his fiftieth birthday.

Through a chance encounter with two young hitchhikers, he learned of healthful diets low in fat and high in fiber, consisting mainly of vegetables and grains.

Although skeptical at first, he began to research and study the possibility of a link between diet and cancer. He decided to give it a try. "This system," he says, "offered me a small spark of hope—a priceless commodity in the face of a death sentence."

Today Dr. Sattilaro acknowledges traditional treatments, but he also now believes that his 100 percent recovery would not have been possible without his drastic change in diet. In his book, *Living Well Naturally,* he describes, in addition to diet guidelines and recipes low in fat and high in fiber, the exercise and stress control program that he followed.

Preventing Colon Cancer

In his book, *The Save Your Life Diet*, Dr. David Rueben states that,

> The United States has the highest rate of cancer of the colon of any country in the world. Cancer of the colon and rectum strikes every five minutes, and every ten minutes, someone dies.

These health problems are mainly attributed to our improper and unhealthy diets.

Obviously, we have a serious national health problem. On the average, people in developing countries who subsist on high fiber diets produce a much larger fecal mass than persons in westernized countries.

This is the principal factor accounting for their fifty times lower prevalence of diverticular disease of the colon, says Dr. Thomas P. Almy, professor of Medicine at Dartmouth Medical School, in *The American Journal of Medicine.*

In February of 1984, the American Cancer Society for the first time made clear recommendations as to a diet that may help prevent cancer. Although their basic recommendations were not as strict as Dr. Sattilaro's, the basics were there:

1. Eat more high-fiber foods such as whole grains, vegetables, and fruits
2. Reduce fat intake
3. Avoid obesity

Doctors now believe that fiber may help protect against cancer of the colon and rectum by speeding fecal matter through the colon. Fiber improves tissue cleansing and thorough elimination. We need plenty of fiber in our diet. Few of us get enough.

Putting Fiber into Your Diet

There are two types of fiber—*crude fiber,* which is *not* water soluble and which cannot be dissolved or liquified, and *dietary fiber,* which *is* water soluble. Both are the indigestible part of plant foods.

Crude fiber moves through the digestive system like a bulldozer, cleansing and sanitizing as it goes. Bran, the most common form of crude fiber, helps solid wastes move through the colon faster and easier.

Dr. Albert Mendeloff of Johns Hopkins Hospital says that by increasing the bulk and speed of waste passing through our systems, we may dilute the cancer-causing substances contained in wastes. Last night's steak, for instance, may not spend enough time in the body's digestive system to be absorbed completely. Therefore, less fat will travel through the arteries, and less fat will be deposited in body cells.

Dietary fiber, the water-soluble fiber, can be found in fruits and vegetables. It promotes cleanliness of the blood and cholesterol level maintenance by acting as a regulator and cleansing sponge. It mops up excesses and impurities that can poison the body and/or clog the arteries. Controlled studies have shown that people on high-fiber vegetarian diets excreted two to three times as much fat or cholesterol as did the people on a low-fiber and meat diet.

Modern food processing methods remove fiber and increase the chance of colon dysfunction. The further we stray from natural, uncooked foods, the greater the risk of colon problems. The best foods are whole grains and raw fruits and vegetables. Nuts, beans, and peas are also excellent sources of fiber.

If you're wondering which foods will supply the fiber you need, see the lists at the end of this chapter.

Adjusting to the Change

In addition to helping colons act more efficiently, these foods promote the growth of a bacteria that actually attacks toxins and eliminates them. By adding both crude and dietary fiber to our diets, we will be promoting smooth and rapid elimination, as well as improving the overall internal cleansing system.

Before you begin overwhelming your body with fiber, I'd like to make you aware of a couple of potential side effects of increasing your fiber consumption. The first is that there is an increased tendency of flatulence (gas). This normally subsides within two to three weeks, as your body adjusts. Chewing your food slowly and thoroughly into a paste before swallowing will help reduce this inconvenience.

The other hazard is the increased risk of clogging the colon temporarily. This can occur when a colon is already somewhat plugged by old and hardened fecal matter or when too much fiber is taken in too quickly—or a combination of these two reasons.

If you do choose to get on the bran wagon, you can certainly improve the results by chewing your food slowly and thoroughly, increasing your fiber consumption gradually over several weeks, and drinking plenty of water.

Unclogging the System

If you are not having at least one large, comfortable bowel movement each day, you have a problem that is undermining your vitality and health—*guaranteed*.

Very few people have thorough bowel function. Dr. John Harvey Kellogg said, "Of the 22,000 operations I have personally performed, I have never found a single, normal colon.'' He maintained that 90 percent of all disease is due to the improper function of the colon.

Fecal matter can remain attached to the bowel walls for days, months, and even years. During my travels, I've had more than one person tell me, "My bowels are in good shape. I have four to five eliminations every day." I am always dismayed to hear this news because consistently frequent eliminations like this are an indication that the colon has collapsed and/or that fecal matter has built up inside the bowel walls. When this happens, many movements are necessary to eliminate through what has probably become a tiny hole about the size of a pencil.

It's our job to reeducate ourselves as to our standards for healthy bowel function and then to follow a healthy regimen to regulate it. Because these principles are vital to our health, let's review them.

The three critical reasons we want to avoid plugging the major highway in our disposal system are:

1. The body can be severely restricted in its ability to assimilate vitamins and minerals.

2. Fecal deposits can cause irritation in the colon and lead to a spastic or inflamed colon, which further interferes with proper bowel function.

3. During the time this fecal matter remains attached to the bowel wall, it continues to decay, producing poisons and toxins that pollute the whole body when they are reabsorbed into the bloodstream. The colon is not stainless steel.

To avoid these risks, it is necessary to increase your consumption of fiber—gradually. Too much too soon can actually promote constipation. Exercising, drinking lots of water, and chewing food thoroughly will also improve the ability of the colon to function efficiently.

Another guideline to remember is to drink no liquids during meals. Proper digestion and elimination begin when saliva interacts with food during chewing. Adding liquids inhibits this important process. No liquid also forces you to chew your food thoroughly. Remember, drink plenty of liquids between meals but *not* during them. Think about me the next time you try to eat a peanut butter sandwich on whole wheat bread without a drink to wash it down!

Laxatives—Helpful or Harmful?

The business of producing laxatives has been around forty to fifty years. It generates an estimated 130 million dollars annually. Obviously, a lot of folks have elimination problems.

But I'm telling you that laxatives rarely need to be used, if at all. They are a stimulant, and the body can easily become dependent on them. Even many herbal laxatives chemically irritate the colon, causing the bowels to move until the laxative, and anything else loose enough to flow out with it, is expelled.

Once the colon has passed any stubborn feces, however, it is unlikely that the colon will be better off than it was before. A colon dependent on laxatives gets lazy, stops working, and gradually becomes weaker and weaker.

In order to create any long-term benefit, we need somehow to soften old, hardened fecal deposits that have attached to the inner walls of the colon and then expel them. The process is slow. It will take a great deal of patience and persistence, but the effects will be long term and thoroughly healthy—unlike those resulting from commercial laxatives.

How to Cleanse and Detoxify Your System

There are three excellent internal cleansing systems I know of that will help draw the toxins and poisons from your body as well as soften, loosen, and expel fecal deposits that may have become attached to the inner colon walls. The first system consists basically of two products: *hydrated bentonite* and *psyllium hulls*.

Hydrated bentonite is a clay water made from volcanic ash. It is an absorbent aid in detoxification and intestinal purification. In the human body a good portion of the toxins and poisons are positively charged. Bentonite has a negative electrical attraction. Because of the minuteness of its particles, it acts like a magnetic sponge, absorbing as much as 200 times its own weight in positively charged toxins as it passes through the digestive tract. The hydrated bentonite draws toxins into the intestinal tract.

Psyllium hulls are the husks of the psyllium seed. When ground, they have two to three times greater bulking capacity than bran fiber or wheat husks. They are smoother and more effective. They absorb toxins and work together with the normal function of the colon to eliminate them.

Internal Cleansing

The second system consists basically of three products: Kalenite, Daily Fiber, and vivalo creme.

Kalenite is a natural cleansing and purifying herbal tablet that forms the core of this internal cleansing program. It contains acacia gum, yellow dock root, plantain, blessed thistle, cloves, red clover, corn silk extract, and butternut bark.

Daily Fiber has been shown to remove toxins, cleanse and purify, increase growth of acidophilus (healthy colon bacteria), and promote colon health. Daily Fiber's synergistic formula contains psyllium husks, guar gum, oat bran, barley malt extract, and fruit pectin.

Vivalo creme is a penetrating olive oil emollient that is applied topically to the abdomen to enhance maximum internal cleansing results. It contains distilled water, olive oil, grain alcohol, lecithin, and agar-agar.

The third system consists of five products that are combined in a powder called *Colon Conditioner*. This powder consists of bentonite, acidophilus (supplies friendly bacteria to the intestinal tract), aloe vera, several natural herbs, and a special fiber blend derived from fruits, grains, and vegetables.

Our highly processed, westernized diet rarely has enough fiber to prevent internal pollution and unnecessary cell degeneration. Consequently, I heartily recommend that either one or a combination of the three internal cleansing systems I've outlined be incorporated into your lifestyle.

Please remember that neither of these cleansing systems will cure any specific disorder. They are for internal cell and colon cleansing. If you have, or suspect you have *any* condition that could be aggravated by these products, consult your physician prior to using them.

Getting Good Results

Many people are concerned about the possibility of becoming addicted to bentonite and psyllium hulls. Let me reassure you that neither of these two products contains any ingredients that could cause addiction. They are natural products that aid the body in doing the best possible job of internal tissue cleansing and detoxification.

The goal is to insure at least one, and preferably two, large, smooth, and pain-free eliminations each day. The main elimination should be from one to three feet long, with a width of somewhere between the width of a teaspoon and a tablespoon. The second elimination of the day would probably be about half the size of the first.

Until your body is producing results like this, your elimination system is not operating at its optimum. These products are designed to help you naturally and consistently achieve this optimum condition.

How to Obtain These Products

I know of two companies that manufacture and distribute their own bentonite and psyllium husks, as well as the other health products. They are:

1. *Nature's Sunshine Products,* P.O. Box 100, Spanish Fork, UT 94660 (801-798-9861).
2. *V.E. Irons, Inc.,* P.O. Box 296, Natick, MA 01760 (617-653-8404).

Each company has a nationwide network of independent distributors. Should you be unable to find a distributor in the phone book, write or call directly to the companies. They will send you literature and/or put their closest distributor in touch with you.

The *Kalenite, Daily Fiber,* and *vivalo creme,* as well as other health products, are manufactured by *Yerba Prima Botanicals,* P.O. Box 2569, Oakland, CA 94614 (415-632-7477).

Colon Conditioner is available in powder or tablet form and can be purchased at your local health food store or fitness center. If they do not carry this product, suggest they contact *Naturade,* 7110 E. Jackson Street, Paramount, CA 90723.

L & H Vitamins, 37-10 Crescent St., Long Island City, NY 11101 (718-937-7400/800-221-1152) is a mail order distributor. Most of the products I've described above can be purchased through them. Call their toll-free number to request a free catalog.

I've purchased products from each of the companies listed above and highly recommend them. Should you decide to look at other, similar products on the market, check the ingredients carefully. Make sure you know each of the ingredients and their functions.

Accentuate the Positive, Eliminate the Negative

The road to higher levels of energy, health, and productivity is a gradually ascending one. Although it has its potholes and setbacks, it *will* take you where you want to go—to improved overall health and high energy levels. This new condition will better equip you to handle the stress and the demands of your fast-paced life.

Too often we think of stress, illness, and disease as things that fall out of the sky—things we "get" rather than things we permit to happen. But, as I hope you're finding out, *we decide our fate by the things we put in and eliminate from our bodies.*

We can no longer blame invisible germs and viruses for our health problems. Even though illness and disease are a risk, we have a good amount of control. We *can* play a major role in creating our own robust and resistive environment.

The more you make proper exercise, vibrant nutrition, and thorough elimination part of your *daily* self-care agenda, the more effectively you create your own strong and resilient internal environment. By creating a lifestyle you can live with, you'll experience the energy, enthusiasm, good health, and ultimate vitality you deserve.

It is essential that you and I use responsibly what helps us and avoid what hinders us in our efforts to feed the fire of life with high octane fuel and to eliminate toxic wastes. They are key ingredients in our search for energy, normal immunity, and high level health. They are living-to-win qualities that help provide us with the resources to live to our fullest God-given capabilities.

Fiber Sources

This list of high-fiber foods will help you choose the best sources of fiber for your diet and lifestyle. Those marked with an asterisk (*) are also low in calories and/or high in nutrition.

High-Fiber Fruits

Apples	Grapefruit
Applesauce (unsweetened)	Oranges

Bananas
Blackberries
Coconut*
Dates
Figs
Grapes

Pears
Peaches
Pineapples
Raspberries
Strawberries
Watermelon

High-Fiber Vegetables

Artichokes*
Asparagus
Avocados
Beans*
Beets
Broccoli*
Brussles Sprouts*
Cabbage
Celery
Carrots
Cauliflower
Corn
Cucumber
Eggplant
Horseradish
Kale Greens

Lentils
Lettuce
Mushrooms
Okra
Parsnips*
Peas
Peppers
Potatoes
Rice, brown
Sauerkraut
Soybeans
Spinach
Squash
Sweet Potatoes
Tomatoes
Turnips*

High-Fiber Nuts and Grains

Almonds
Barley
Bran, cereal*
Bran, wheat*
Bread, rye
Bread, whole wheat

Cereals, wheat
Graham crackers
Oatmeal
Peanuts
Wheat Germ

12

The Best Alternative

What is the most powerful, positive alternative to the pressures we face every day? You may be surprised at the answer.

Exercise is the best method of breaking any destructive lifestyle pattern. When we are truly searching for an alternative to prepare us to handle the tensions of our normal day, consistent exercise is the solution that will help us normalize and chemically balance our body.

The healthiest individuals run from the "quick fixes" that actually hinder them and move to positive habits, like exercise, as an alternative that will help them. While actually reducing overall wear and tear, exercise also prepares you to optimize your day to day challenges *and* opportunities. Exercise is not the best alternative for all people all of the time. But it is the best one for most people most of the time!

The Best Medicine

No single option available has a greater impact than exercise on our ability to prevent, manage, and alleviate the behavioral disorders to which human beings are subject. Granted, other factors—good nutrition, counseling, seminars, proper elimination, etc.—are also important. But without exercise they will not have the overall positive effect on health, longevity, and your God-given potential.

It is a clinical fact that without adequate exercise we die prematurely. We simply do not function at our optimum—mentally, physically, or spiritually—without exercise.

Let's use the honey bee as an example. The bee is a highly efficient flying machine that soon folds its wings and takes it easy when put in a zero gravity environment. At first it appears to enjoy the free ride, but within a few days it weakens and dies.

Our human bodies need to struggle. Two decades ago as we began to explore outer space, the human body experienced weightlessness for the first time and confirmed our need for physical exertion. Without gravity to promote exercise, blood pressure increased and cardio-respiratory efficiency decreased. Along with the loss of muscle tone, these are the major symptoms of aging. In weightlessness, one step beyond no-exercise, the function of the body is omitted. As scientists soon discovered, the human body grows old very quickly during prolonged periods of weightlessness.

Hippocrates, the father of medicine, recognized this and considered exercise the best medicine. Without it, he proposed, bodies suffered from muscular atrophy (the slow wasting away of muscle tissue) and premature death.

A healthy muscle is long and lean. Exercise enthusiasts develop it in their pursuit of the "long, lean, and mean machine." A short, squat muscle, nearly saturated with intramuscular fat, is what a neglected muscle can come to look like. With exercise, fatty muscles can be converted into sleek, well-toned muscles. Anyone who can exercise can prevent or reverse the process of muscle atrophy and premature death.

Sitting it Out

We spend approximately two-thirds of our life in positions that compress or shorten our stature. The other third is spent in a relatively neutral position—lying down. We can use alternative positions that will decompress and lengthen our stature—positions that will prevent unnecessary back problems and thus help reduce unnecessary degeneration.

Sitting is one of the most destructive postures humans ever learned, and it needn't be such a predominant posture. In years past, people would sit occasionally to rest their feet; now we stand occasionally to rest our seats! Our sedentary lifestyles effectively reduce the amount of oxygen available to the entire body, which causes us to function far below our optimum capacity.

The conventional way of sitting bends the body at a ninety degree angle. This unnatural angle is one of the major contributing factors to most common back ailments. It encourages the bent-forward, huddled position that compresses the discs in the lower back. It cramps internal organs, restricts free breathing, and inhibits blood circulation. Sitting this way is a double negative:

> First, it requires at least twice the energy to hold the huddled position.
> Second, it restricts the two main bodily functions that deliver energy throughout the system— breathing and blood circulation.

I'm convinced that if we replaced all the nonessential conventional chairs with step stools, and raised our tables and desks so we could stand, we'd be healthier. And we'd measurably increase our productivity as a nation. Do yourself a favor—sit only when it's necessary, and get up often to stretch.

Back chairs are a nice alternative to the usual chairs we are accustomed to sitting in. Because they promote better s less energy to function. Similar to bending to restrict or stop the flow of water, poor posture restricts blood circulation.

The forward slanting seat and supportive leg cushion of the back chair distributes your body weight to align your spine in its proper position. This puts less strain on your back, neck, and shoulder muscles, improves circulation, and helps you get the most out of your potential energy.

There are several models of these chairs available, and most office furniture stores carry them.

Stretching Your Way to the Top

Sweden is far ahead of us in this appreciation of healthy sitting and stretching. Bars secured across the top of doorways are commonplace. People routinely get up from their desks and gently hang by their hands. This practice gives their back and spine a relieving stretch.

Americans are just beginning to catch on to this trend to reduce pressure and prevent fatigue. Bob Hope recently commented that he's been doing this for years. He feels it has contributed to his good health and longevity.

All of the stretching movements I will suggest interrelate and complement the aerobics I will soon be recommending. They are simple and can be done at almost any moment of the day.

These *stretchercises* have helped thousands feel more relaxed, energetic, creative, and productive. In the appendix I have provided instructions for relaxers, stretchercises, and flexercises. I'm confident that you will find some that will help offset the side effects of our sedentary lifestyles.

Embarrassing Figures

I'm convinced that our sedentary lifestyle has helped contribute to our rising illness-related expenses. Look at the trends. In 1950, Americans were spending $12 billion on health care. In 1986 it was $465.4 billion. In 1989 it is expected to exceed $511 billion.

I firmly believe that the greatest impact on these appalling and embarrassing figures will come from how well you and I are willing to take care of ourselves. Our number one option, the one likeliest to keep the demands placed upon us at a healthy and productive level, is exercise.

We're beginning to see some response to the problem from the business world. Many corporations have instituted exercise programs for their employees. Dr. Dennis Colacino, director of PepsiCo's fitness programs, says that implementing an exercise program into the organization made employees "happier, healthier, more alert, and more productive."

Few people realize it, but business and industry now spend in excess of $250 billion each year on illness and injury care. The average cost per employee for health care today exceeds $2,000. Absenteeism during 1984 alone cost business over $825 million. Sedentary employees have an average of 30 percent more hospital days per year than exercisers.

In the state of Minnesota, heart disease alone accounts for approximately one million lost work days, $14 million in replacement costs, and $162 million in disability payments. The common backache costs U.S. businesses an estimated $10 billion in workman's compensation, $19 billion in absenteeism, and another one billion dollars in lost productivity.

In Search of Executive Health

More and more executives are motivated to fight the onset of premature diseases. They like to feel they are in control of their lives and their jobs. That control, they are realizing, depends heavily upon their health. Intellectually, they have concluded that less than optimum health affects their performance. They look at good health as another goal to reach—a goal that will give consistent and long term payoffs.

A good friend of mine, Rick Andrews, told me he doesn't have the time to exercise, but he is convinced of its value—so he's decided to hire someone to do it for him. Obviously, Rick said this in jest. But as much as we'd like to, we cannot delegate this task; neither should we put it off. The consequences are too dire and the benefits too great.

Currently one-third to one-half of all U.S. companies now sponsor physical fitness programs ranging from exercise sessions in on-site facilities to running teams and arrangements with nearby health clubs and YMCAs. Top management is finding that after initiation of a fitness program, overall company health care and insurance costs have decreased dramatically, absenteeism among employees who exercise regularly is substantially lower, turnover has decreased, and productivity has dramatically increased.

In the September 14, 1987 edition of *USA Today,* futurists predict that by the year 2000 virtually all U.S. companies will be offering programs to employees that promote fitness/wellness.

Exercise, combined with education, can be as effective as surgery in ninety-five out of one hundred back problems. Imagine the difference that could make to thousands and thousands of people in pain, as well as reducing the amount U.S. businesses spend on back problems—nearly $30 billion—each year.

And imagine the difference exercise and fitness could make to American business. The Fitness Institute Bulletin reports:

> A corporation with a 50-member management staff that pays little attention to physical fitness will be set back at least $300,000 annually in lost productivity, efficiency, absenteeism, and job turnovers. If health promotion programs could

conservatively cut these costs one-third, the corporation would save $100,000.

What Will It Do for You?

When your body reacts to the demands placed upon it, the energy produced travels to the muscles, where it is absorbed. This is what causes the tension. In years past, lifestyles that contained much physical activity helped rid muscles of excess tension.

Our present lifestyles involve much less activity than past generations. We sit watching TV or working at a desk. We just sit there and get sick. Our twentieth-century lifestyle has eliminated 90 percent of the physical activity and exercise our bodies need to operate efficiently. (Remember the honey bee?)

We live in an age of fast food and slow burn. Exercise is the most effective alterative in helping us maintain healthier cholesterol levels by allowing us to burn off excess fats and sugars. Our ability to digest and metabolize food, as well as to eliminate waste by-products, is enhanced.

Exercise can actually help reduce high blood pressure, thus lessening the risk of heart disease and stroke. With exercise, the bones get stronger, the aging process is slowed, the appetite is controlled, and the ability to relax is improved. When we exercise, we feel better and are less likely to get sick.

An Excellent Anti-Depressant

Exercise can help us become more mentally fit, too. It has been shown to counteract anxiety and depression, improve mental capacities, and increase self-esteem. Experiments conducted by Dr. John M. Griest and colleagues showed that depression could be controlled and/or alleviated with running. Their results compared favorably with those received from patients in psychotherapy and those taking anti-depressant medication.

Dr. Thaddeus Kostrubala, a San Francisco-based psychiatrist and researcher, reports that when he began running with his patients three times a week, "Funny things began to happen." Patients who had been labeled paranoid schizophrenic began showing signs of immense improvement. In fact, they showed signs of completely reversing their own symptoms.

"That," he says, "was the beginning of my excitement, because I had never seen anything like it. It didn't make sense. It violated the definition of the disease. Ever since, I have been using running as a therapeutic tool."

Rubbing Out Stress

In its effect on the body, massage is actually a close relative of exercise. It is also related to relaxation. Massage is a relaxing form of exercise and a physically stimulating form of relaxation that is not self-initiated.

Technically, massage is a variety of systematic and scientific manipulations of bodily tissues. A skilled massage therapist uses his or her hands to affect the nervous and muscular systems and the general circulation. Massage has been around for centuries—Hippocrates advocated the practice—and it is gaining popularity.

Some myths still remain. We may conjure up images of a muscle-bound masseur kneading a writhing victim on a table. Or we may associate it with something "sleazy"—the old "massage parlour" image. Some people fear letting a stranger handle their bodies while they are partially clothed and in what would seem to be a vulnerable posture.

A new method of massage is performed on a clothed, seated client and uses no oils. Called "on-site massage," it lasts thirty minutes or less and helps relieve the tensions of a stressful day. The most popular on-site method is a 1500 year-old Japanese massage technique called *Amma*. Unlike the Swedish massage, the Amma method leaves you feeling invigorated and energetic.

As the myths are shattered with accurate information, more and more people are enjoying the marvelous health-promoting benefits of massage. Its positive effects are numerous; following is a partial list. Massage:

- Reduces stress—both physical and mental
- Restores lost energy
- Releases tension
- Speeds muscle recovery after heavy exercise
- Increases cardiovascular and lymph circulation
- Aids digestion and elimination
- Improves muscle tone
- Speeds healing of broken bones, torn ligaments, and some forms of temporary paralysis
- Rejuvenates the body cosmetically
- Increases body awareness
- Feels good

Many physicians, including those in orthopedics, neurology, psychiatry, and geriatrics, now consider massage an important technique to be used in conjunction with medical therapy. A qualified massage therapist can help restore function to muscles and joints, improve circulation and general body tone, and provide relief of mental and physical fatigue.

It is recommended that the massage therapist be one who has received training, has graduated from a recognized, licensed, approved school of massage, and is an active member of the American Massage and Therapy Association (AMTA). These individuals have been schooled in anatomy, physiology, massage, hydrotherapy, hygiene, and professional ethics.

How can you find a reliable massage therapist? Many clubs, spas, and health studios offer massage. Or you may consider contacting a therapist who has an office practice. Talk to friends; or call ATMA at (312) 761-AMTA. But do try massage as a natural and positive alternative to enhance whole-body health.

Want to Feel Better?

Physically fit people—those who exercise regularly—will tend to eat properly, manage time more wisely, recognize their own stress symptoms, get the sleep they need, and stop smoking—all without consciously planning to do so. It's even true that individuals who exercise often earn more money than unfit persons.

The vice president at Robert Half, a personnel and recruiting consultants firm, says: "Physically-active people often appear more confident, competitive, energetic, and self-reliant. And employers pay a premium for these qualities."

Harvard and Stanford University studies report that even modest exercise helps prolong life. It's not clear yet how much time exercisers add to their life spans. But it *does* make a difference. Regular exercise:

- Decreases or stops osteoporosis
- Temporarily raises blood temperature, which enhances purification
- Helps conditioned people endure stress more readily
- Can help you feel happier, more energetic, healthier, and more productive
- Helps prevent alcohol and drug abuse
- Enhances alcoholic and drug rehabilitation

In general, regular exercise helps you *feel* better due to internal chemical changes.

Reducing Life's Wear and Tear

Make responsible use of an exercise program tailored to fit your needs, and the return will be a greater capacity to manage stress along with better health and peak productivity. You will also find that exercise can help reduce the wear and tear that stress has on your body. You will be more resilient to life's traumas, better able to bounce back after high pressure situations, and better able to react with calm objectivity.

More and more people are joining you in this. More and more people want to feel they are in control.

Sue Halloran is just one example of thousands upon thousands of people who use regular exercise to make a healthy difference in their lives. Here is her testimony:

> I used to be a professional dancer. Then I injured myself and had a number of back surgeries. The pain I had almost continuously showed in my face.
>
> It's been a long road back to health, and a number of tools have helped me to recover. One of the most important has certainly been exercise, which I do regularly. I schedule it as I would an appointment with a client. I won't let myself break it, just as I wouldn't break a client's appointment. Without exercise I just don't feel as good about myself.
>
> Now I look younger and feel better than I did seven years ago. We have an idea that getting old means getting decrepit and losing our health. If I went from four to thirty-four becoming healthier, perhaps as I go from thirty-four to forty-four and forty-four to fifty-four I'll become healthier yet!

Turning Your Health Around

Recently I was presenting a seminar, and I informed the participants that someone thirty pounds overweight can get an idea how much extra poundage that is by lifting two men's bowling balls, one in each hand. *That's* overweight!

A critically overweight gentleman with a sense of humor interrupted, "I must be carrying bowling balls for the whole team!'' Extra weight is an enormous burden; it is second only to smoking as a promoter of illness.

One in four men suffer from ''Dunlaps disease.'' That's when his stomach dun-laps over his belt.

Let's take Morgan Kramer, a forty-three-year-old Citicorp executive vice president as an example of how extra weight can affect the body—and what can be done to correct the situation. When I met him, Morgan was working sixty to seventy hours a week, carrying thirty extra pounds, and not exercising at all. He had begun to notice that it was increasingly easy for him to get irritated with minor annoyances. He had difficulty sleeping, and his energy level was consistently low.

''I began to realize my health had deteriorated,'' Morgan told me. ''The thought of a heart attack crossed my mind. Out of panic, I talked to my doctor and asked how I could improve my health and definitely prevent a heart attack. I look back now, and I'm grateful my doctor was pro-exercise. He started me walking and, later, cycling and jogging.''

Morgan's heart-rate initially measured at ninety beats per minute. Today, less than a year later, it's down to sixty. He's lost thirty pounds, looks great, and feels wonderful. Morgan sleeps fine, and his personality, by his own admission, has changed for the better. Even the quantity and quality of his work has improved. Exercise, he wholeheartedly believes, was the catalyst for the exciting turnaround.

Why not experience your optimum health? Why not test the boundaries of your abilities? You can feel better and achieve more of what you want. If you, like me, feel the desire always to be at your optimum capacity, then let's look at some exercise action steps to get you there.

13
Where the Action Is

Exercise has been credited with positively affecting sexual fulfillment, helping to make pregnancies healthier, and assisting in alleviating depression. There's no telling what great things it will do for you!

I certainly hope you're excited about all the benefits you're going to experience from regular exercise. Aerobic conditioning is the key to efficient circulation of blood and oxygen. Exercise is imperative to high energy levels, productivity, and the prevention of premature aging.

What is Aerobic Exercise?

Air, water, and food are essential to life—in that order. They are your three most powerful energy resources. Exercise is the catalyst that helps combine these elements and enables the human body to make the most of its potential.

If you don't exercise, you're not making the most of the power available to you. The resulting situation is something like a 300 horsepower automobile idling in the driveway; until you get out on the highway you can't utilize your full potential.

When I speak of exercise, I mean more than shopping, doing household chores, caring for the children, walking to and from the car, or getting up from the chair to turn the TV channel. I'm not even referring to diversionary exercises such as bowling, gardening, waterskiing, or taking a stroll. These activities are important, of course. They help you relax and gently release your body from the pressures of the day.

It is *aerobic* exercise, however, that produces healthful and life-changing results. Aerobic exercise produces the most benefit in the least amount of time. Correct aerobic exercise is *pro* stress; it places a health-promoting demand on the body. Aerobic exercise is any activity that produces an increased heart-rate with the *intensity, frequency,* and *duration* to stimulate cardiovascular conditioning.

This conditioning takes place when the demands placed upon the body are enough to stimulate the heart and lungs to deliver optimum levels of oxygen to the working muscles and cells. Muscles are challenged to become efficient at absorbing the maximum amount of oxygen from the blood. The level of fitness is determined by how efficient the heart and lungs are at delivering oxygen and how efficient the muscles and cells are at utilizing it.

Before starting any exercise program, have your health checked thoroughly by your doctor. If you are over thirty-five and have been inactive for some time, a physical stress test is a wise choice. By the time people reach the age of thirty-five, they have too often been exercising little more than caution. Regardless of your exercise habits until now, begin exercising slowly, and always consistently monitor your pulse.

How Much is Enough?

How do we make sure our exercise is intense enough to achieve aerobic conditioning? When the heartbeats per minute (bpm) reach and remain within what is called the "training zone," we are experiencing aerobic conditioning.

For most people, this zone is over 100 beats per minute. Depending on your age, there is a range of thirty to fifty heartbeats between the low and high end of the training zone.

To figure your personal training zone, you will need to calculate the correct and healthy number of times your heart should beat per minute *during* the exercise session. First, subtract your age from 220. This will give you your maximum bpm.

Now multiply that figure by first 65 percent and then 85 percent to get the respective low and high bpm for your body.

Let's use a forty-year-old person as an example:

$$220 - 40 = 180$$
$$180 \times 65\% = 117 \text{ (minimum beats per minute)}$$
$$180 \times 85\% = 153 \text{ (maximum beats per minute)}$$

Keep in mind that if you are taking medication for heart and blood vessel disease, this formula may not apply. Consult your physician.

Once you have arrived at these figures, you can determine your own personal training zone and then work to attain it during exercise.

How to Reach Your Goal

Once you have decided to work toward your training zone, let me provide some useful information to help you accomplish your goal. Stay closer to the low end of your training zone (minimum bpm), and move gradually toward the high end (maximum bpm) as your physical condition improves. People in *good* physical condition should be able to add another ten beats to the high end of their training zone without harm.

Your body will experience the greatest level of benefit after the first ten minutes of exercise and up to another thirty minutes. Of course, the benefits after that time continue but in diminishing amounts.

People starting on exercise programs tend to overdo it; then they feel worn out and discouraged. My advice is to begin with a manageable five to ten minutes of exercise, then progress to twenty to thirty. Consistently exercising for twenty to thirty minutes will give you the most benefits with the least effort.

Exercise three to five times each week. Keep up the momentum without overworking yourself.

When your personal exercise program has the intensity, duration, and frequency to achieve aerobic conditioning, you are best prepared to realize the benefits I discussed earlier: reduced risk of degenerative disease, controlled appetite, improved ability to relax, increased mental capacity and alertness, improved self-esteem—I could go on, but that should be enough to get you started with the right attitude.

Remember, you do not have to experience excruciating pain to get into physical condition or to maintain it. Too much exercise becomes distressing and painful—a destructive demand that can produce unhealthy results. Crash exercise programs are about as effective as crash diets and probably even more dangerous.

Take it easy. When the intensity of your exercise is increased gradually and consistently, you will experience very little pain. In fact, you may be surprised to find out exercise can be pleasant!

The All-Important Pulse Check

Your heart-rate is the best inside story of your body's reaction to physical demands. It is the mirror of your body's metabolism. If you ever join a group exercise program that does not emphasize heart-rate monitoring, I suggest that you find out why immediately and perhaps find a program that does.

Checking the pulse of your heart is an easy method of evaluating your present physical condition. There is a pulse each time your heart beats.

The average resting pulse is seventy to seventy-five, with women typically having higher rates than men. As we discussed earlier, our sedentary lifestyle contributes to this average. A healthier average would be at least ten to fifteen beats slower.

Regular exercisers condition their hearts. When your heart has been conditioned, it can take in and pump out more blood per beat than a sedentary person's heart can. The conditioned heart doesn't have to work as hard. It is very common for consistently-exercising individuals to lower their heart rates by at least ten beats per minute.

Reducing our heart-rates by just ten beats per minute adds up to 600 fewer beats per hour and 14,400 fewer beats each day. That reduction becomes significant when you consider that at an average of seventy beats per minute, your heart beats in excess of 100,000 times every twenty-four hours! Imagine your heart being able to pump its daily average of nearly 2000 gallons of blood—at the rate of six quarts per minute—through 60,000 miles of blood vessels, nourishing 75 trillion cells with oxygen—all with 14,400 fewer beats!

Studies have clearly shown a link between lower heart-rates and the reduced risk of heart disease. A Northwestern Medical School study found that men with resting heart-rates of sixty or fewer beats per minute had two to three times less chance of dying from coronary heart disease than did men whose resting heart-rates were above eighty.

Determining Your Average Resting Pulse

Determining your average resting pulse will have to be accomplished over several days. The best time to check your pulse is before you get out of bed each morning. Find the pulse beneath your lower jaw or on the upper inside of your wrist. You will be able to detect the faint beat with your first or second index finger. Don't use your thumb because it's not as sensitive as other fingers and can have its own beat; this could affect the accuracy of your measurement.

Count the number of beats for ten seconds and multiply that number by six. If you're not in a hurry, you can count the beats for the entire sixty seconds. Your pulse, of course, will vary depending on your "condition." Stress, physical activity, medication, temperature, and altitude all affect the pulse rate. You can also expect a quickened pulse after drinking alcohol or coffee or after smoking.

Once you are sure of your average pulse rate, evaluate it, based on the following chart:

Heart BPM	Heart Condition
Less than 50	Athletic
50-60	Excellent
61-70	Good
71-80	Average
81-90	Fair
91-100	Poor
100+	Dangerous

Keep in mind that heartbeats can be misleading. Low heart-rates can be related to factors such as drugs you are taking, heart ailments, and metabolic and genetic makeup. Without exercise, a slower-than-average heart-rate cannot be interpreted to mean the health of the heart is above average. Only exercise can assure you of that.

Likewise, high heart-rates don't necessarily mean what you may think. After you begin an exercise program, you may find that your average rate is ten or more beats higher than the average resting pulse. Most likely that means you are over-training. Slow down a little.

Once you have begun exercising, take your pulse immediately after the strenuous part of your program. If the intensity of the exercise is correct, your pulse will be somewhere within your training zone. If at any time during an exercise session you suspect that your heart-rate is exceeding your training zone, slow down immediately to check. If it is, decrease the intensity of your workout. Remember, overuse is abuse.

How's Your Heart?

After a workout, your heart-rate will be briefly accelerated. The rate at which it returns to its normal bpm is called your "heart recovery rate." Monitoring this will give you an indication of how healthy your heart is. With a little practice, you'll be able to measure it easily and accurately.

Immediately after exercise, take your pulse for six seconds and multiply the figure by ten. Exactly one minute later, repeat the procedure. Subtract the second rate from the first; then divide by ten. This figure is your recovery rate.

For example, say your exercise pulse is 145, and after one minute your pulse is down to 105. 145 minus 105 is forty, and forty divided by ten is four. That number falls into the good range, as the chart indicates. Note that the higher the number, the healthier the heart.

Recovery Rate	Rating
Higher than 6	Super
4-6	Excellent
3-4	Good
2-3	Fair
Less than 2	Poor

The test I have just described will not necessarily reveal any other problem a heart might have, but it is generally true that the faster the heart recovers from exercise, the healthier it is.

Starting Your Exercise Routine

Now let's discuss the more formal and structured program of aerobic exercise—the foundation of long-term energy, health, and productivity.

Remember, exercise is the natural last phase of the daily demands placed upon our bodies. It counteracts our daily inertia, uses the energy produced as a result of our reactions to the stimuli of the day and our lack of movement, and releases the pressures and tensions of the day. Without physical activity, energy and chemicals accumulate inside our bodies and cause numerous health problems. Your body can become something like a volcano waiting to explode.

Exercise, especially aerobic exercise, makes good use of this energy. It also provides a relaxing diversion from the problems and pressures of work and life itself. As we begin to explore some of the various forms of aerobic exercise, I'd like to remind you again to begin slowly. When it's overdone, what you took up for your health's sake you may give up for your body's sake! When you start a regimented aerobics program, however, you may be surprised that the exercise you once considered a tremendous burden and tiresome duty can become a nice diversion from the pressures of your day.

There are four important stages during exercise. Following these steps will help insure that you experience the full value of your investment. The steps are, in order, pre warm-up, warm-up, aerobic conditioning, and cool down.

Pre Warm-Up

Prepare for your exercise. Avoid all food during the two hours before exercise. This will insure that your blood and energy reserves can be used in your muscles instead of being diverted to the process of digestion.

Two to three glasses of unpolluted water are needed to provide your body with the essential liquids it needs during strenuous activity. Consume them within two to three hours of your exercise session. The last water should be consumed one-half to one hour beforehand. This will generally give you an opportunity to relieve yourself of what your body doesn't need before you exercise.

Warm-Up

This phase safely warms the body and prepares it for exercise. A few minutes of walking and/or calisthenics followed by *light* stretching will improve your body's flexibility and reduce the risk of injury to your muscles, ligaments, tendons, and joints.

Aerobic Conditioning

Once pre warm-up and warm-up are completed, you are ready to begin aerobic exercise. These twenty to thirty minutes of aerobics will give you the most benefit for the least time and effort.

The latest research says we don't have to stay in our training zone continuously during this period. In fact, we now know that more effective conditioning can be accomplished when the training is accompanied by intermittent "slow down" periods.

For example, jog in the training zone for ten minutes. Walk for one or two minutes. Jog another ten, walk for two, and then jog for ten. The total amount of aerobic conditioning time is still thirty minutes, but the brief slow down periods actually make the session *more* effective than thirty continuous minutes in your training zone.

Cool-Down

After a work out, the cool-down period eases the body back to a normal pace. Your body's metabolism cannot stop as abruptly as you can stop exercising. It will continue to produce chemicals that can cause cramps and sore muscles if you do not slow down gradually enough for your body to slow down with you.

During this cool-down period the body is still warm and flexible; that's when it will be most receptive to stretching. You will get far better results and have far less chance of a stretching injury when you stretch while you are "warm" versus cold.

The cool-down period is a good opportunity to replenish lost body fluids. Drink plenty of water. You may find that eating fruit, especially melons, are helpful. They are quickly absorbed by your body, replenish fluids, supply quick energy, and taste great.

What's Right for You?

There are many different kinds of exercise—for strength, rhythm, relaxation, and flexibility. But I believe that when *aerobic conditioning* is included in any exercise plan it will have the greatest impact on your overall health. Your job is to select the combination of exercises that you'll enjoy or—even more important—exercises that you'll *do*.

Activities such as chopping wood, skating, tennis, dancing, sex, downhill skiing, golf, strolling, bowling, and gardening are considered primarily as diversion exercises because they lack the intensity and duration to keep your heart rate in the training zone.

Let's take a look at some of the most rewarding and beneficial forms of aerobic conditioning. Of course the intensity and duration of the exercise determines its placement as much or more than the exercise itself does.

The best aerobic exercises in descending order are: cross-country skiing, swimming, rebounding, rowing, running/jogging, cycling, brisk walking, jumping rope, chair stepping, running in place, jumping jacks.

Cross-Country Skiing: The Ideal Aerobic Exercise

Cross-country skiing comes closest to the most ideal aerobic exercise.

In a ten year study of 21,000 people, well-known fitness authority Kenneth Cooper, M.D., concluded that of all aerobic exercises cross-country skiing is best because the skiing motion uses nearly all of the major muscles in a smooth, rhythmic motion. It's easy to learn and relatively inexpensive. It also gives you a chance to enjoy the beauty of snowy landscapes and make the most of what could be a dreary winter!

Cross-country skiing has proven to be very effective and compatible in the rehabilitation of injuries to the feet, knees, legs, and back. Many doctors feel that it is a safe enough exercise to be used for cardiovascular rejuvenation; they actually prescribe it to patients.

Until the mid-seventies cross-country skiing generated little interest. Now it is estimated that more than one million pairs of skis are being used in the United States today. Major cross country ski centers and trail networks are sprouting up everywhere. Many downhill resorts offer cross-country skiing as well.

Cross-country skiing is convenient. Forget about ski lifts and prepared slopes; all you need is snow. And it's easy to learn. Practically anybody who can walk can also ski. Have a skiing friend get you started. Or take a sixty to ninety minute lesson.

Once you're hooked, you can probably rent skis, boots, and poles for the day. Should you decide to purchase your own equipment, you can be nicely outfitted for around $200. Whether you rent or buy, cross-country skiing lets you completely avoid expensive lift tickets. Your chances of injury are also about one-twentieth compared with downhill skiers. Cross-country skiers set their own speeds.

Your outings will give you the opportunity to enjoy winter-time nature. Many of today's avid skiers had little good to say about the season until they put on their caps and gloves, got out, and skied. Many actually look forward to snow flurries! Besides the joys of nature, you'll also have ample opportunity to meet new people and enjoy social get-togethers.

Interested in taking a cross-country ski vacation? Contact Cross Country Ski Areas of America, P. O. Box 557, Brattleboro, VT 05301. They can provide you with a directory of registered commercial ski areas.

For those who live in a tropical climate but wish to ski year round, want to get in shape for skiing, or desire the physiological benefits of skiing without going outdoors, the ski machine may be the answer. The ski machine simulates the rhythm and movement of skiing. Weather is no longer a factor, and the chance of injuries virtually disappears.

I am aware of two companies that manufacture excellent ski simulators. To get information and prices call *Nordic Track* at 800-328-5888 (in Minnesota, (612) 448-6987; in Canada, 800-433-9582) or *Fitness Master* at 800-328-8995 (in Minnesota, (612) 474-0992; in Canada, 800-665-4872).

Cross-country skiing—whether done indoors or outdoors—provides you with the best aerobic conditioning with the least wear and tear to the body.

Swimming: The Anti-Aging Exercise

One strong swimming advocate, Paul Hutinger, Ph.D., holds that swimming is "the closest thing we have to an anti-aging formula."

For years swimming has maintained its reputation as an ideal exercise. When asked "What's the best exercise?" most people would quickly respond, "Swimming!" Although cross-country skiing is now considered the most efficient aerobic exercise, swimming is still a close second. It does not place quite the demand on the major muscle groups, nor does it involve as many muscles as skiing does. But it does have an anti-aging effect.

One of the greatest advantages of swimming is that it produces very little distress on the body compared to many other forms of exercise, yet it has equal or greater benefits. For instance, it doesn't carry the risk of tennis elbow, blisters, or sprained ankles. Swimmers experience significantly less bone, joint, and muscle problems than joggers, tennis players, racquetball enthusiasts, or soccer players.

The buoyancy created by water enables the swimmer to weigh about 90 percent less than normal. Consequently, the exercise done in water seems easier, but the body works harder because of the water's resistance. Some scientific evidence shows that we can maintain efficient cardio-respiratory conditioning by swimming twice a week for only fifteen to twenty-five minutes each time.

Water exercise can be extremely therapeutic for physical rehabilitation. People with back, muscle, or joint problems can easily get into and keep up an efficient exercise program. You can, too. Whether it is your primary choice for conditioning or an adjunct, swimming is an excellent aerobic exercise that will produce a high level of conditioning with a minimum of distress to the body.

Rowing: Major Muscle Workout

The United States Rowing Association (U.S.R.A.) reports that an ever-increasing number of men and women are enjoying rowing. It "ranks among the most physiologically demanding of any aerobic sports, with cross-country skiing being its only parallel" (Ohio University exercise physiologist Fredrick C. Hagerman, Ph.D.).

Rowing exercises both the upper and lower halves of the body while elevating the pulse rate into the target zone. All the major muscles and most of the body's minor muscle groups get a good workout, increasing strength and endurance. As an added benefit, rowing outdoors can be scenic, peaceful, and relaxing. Most boat clubs offer lessons. Your involvement may range from recreational to racing. Once you've developed the expertise, you should be able to rent the boat of your choice. Check your telephone directory for the nearest club, or write to U.S.R.A., 4 Boathouse Row, Philadelphia, PA 19130.

Although you sacrifice fresh air and a scenic lake or river view, you may prefer the rowing machine to actual boating. While providing the same physiological benefits, it eliminates the need for life preservers and removes the worry about weather. A good unit can be purchased from most fitness stores.

Jogging: Most Popular Aerobic Exercise

Jogging is probably the most popular aerobic conditioner today. In 1968 there were only an estimated 100,000 joggers in the United States. Today we're 30 million strong. Kenneth H. Cooper, M.D., helped introduce the jogging boom that first exploded in the early seventies. He virtually invented the word aerobics as we know it. Cooper and his co-workers have scientifically shown us how to measure the results of exercise and determine our level of fitness. This system of measure can also help us make exercising much, much safer.

People jog to lose weight, become fit, reduce the effects of stress, lower the risk of heart disease, and fight depression.

Jogging is easy. It requires no special equipment, and it doesn't cost anything. You can get started right away. Purchase a good pair of running shoes and clothes appropriate for the weather, lean forward, and get going.

Jogging is, simply, a slowed form of running. The kind of jogging I recommend is the *slow* form. You should be able to carry on a relatively normal conversation with a partner at this pace.

Keep in mind that you should stretch only mildly before starting. The body will still be "cold" and resistent. First walk, then jog slowly and increase your speed gradually as you warm up. Jog at the level your current condition permits. Maintain that level for the duration you have already chosen. Monitor your heart-rate to insure that you are not moving beyond your training zone. Afterward, cool down. Walk for three to five minutes and then stretch. Your body will respond better now that you've warmed up.

Don't overdo it. If you jog more than three miles a day, five days a week, you are jogging more than you need to. In fact, as you increase the miles over fifteen per week, the rate of increased fitness decreases rapidly and the rate of injury increases at the same accelerated rate. Jogging three times a week for twenty to thirty minutes within your training zone is a healthy medium.

The human biological machine is designed for movement. The whole body, like any individual organ, is made to be used. Second only to walking, running is the most natural and the easiest form of exercise that will enable you to be mentally and physically fit. Men and women, young and old—all types of people run to be fit. You can, too.

Cycling: The Stress-Free Exercise

Cycling is another form of exercise that has become very popular. Bicycles and exercise cycle sales are booming.

Bicycling is also a relatively painless and stress-free exercise that has appeal for young and old alike. It is basically painless because of its fluid motion. Bikers enjoy the benefits of aerobic conditioning without the wear-and-tear associated with some exercises. Biking gradually increases one's fitness level, but it doesn't require a great level of ability. Almost anyone can bike.

Like many of the other exercises we have discussed, cycling can be enjoyed indoors and outdoors. More and more

I see bikers in their fifties, sixties, and seventies. Bikers are becoming increasingly aware that cycling can improve their quality of life by improving their fitness levels. Remember, however, that if you are interested in developing more arm strength, biking will not do it.

The outdoor cyclist has the advantages of sunshine, fresh air, and the beauty of nature. In addition, biking clubs offer the opportunity to socialize as well as a chance to take part in organized scenic trips. One-day outings can have the effect of a whole vacation! Longer outdoor excursions can occur over several days. Group members tour national parks and visit points of interest.

Indoor biking can be tempting if you value convenience, privacy, and an opportunity to read, listen to music, or watch TV. Indoor stationary bicycles, of course, don't subject the biker to the extremes of weather. Consequently, the enthusiast can make a commitment to stay aerobically fit year round. The scenery can become boring, but the convenience can't be beat.

Most fitness stores have a good selection of cycling machines. Many are now designed to help you condition the upper body also, giving them an advantage over the outdoor bicycle.

Walking: The Overlooked Exercise

Walking is often overlooked as a form of exercise. When done briskly, walking offers all the benefits of other aerobic exercises, plus some advantages all its own. It's an excellent way to begin an exercise program. Plus, you already know how to do it, you're virtually always dressed for it, and you can go places on your way to becoming healthier. Seldom will you have to change clothes or shower afterward. You won't even have to get in your car to drive somewhere to do it. Exercise on your way to the store, the bus stop, the office, etc.

Walking, of course, will not produce the benefits of jogging as quickly, but the risk of injury and soreness is lowered considerably.

Walking has been used successfully in weight control—even when the subject's normal eating habits were not modified! In a California study, subjects lost an average of twenty-two pounds during the year—even though their food intake often increased. Walking's success as part of an exercise program can probably be attributed to its stress-free nature. People keep at it diligently because they enjoy it. Often they can be induced to begin a more ambitious program.

An ever-growing number of people are walking. They walk during their lunch breaks, for instance. Instead of the proverbial eat and run, they now eat and walk. Walking provides an escape—a chance to get away for awhile—and helps eliminate that "lazy" feeling after eating. It can be a convenient and relaxing way to conduct business. Most people are coordinated enough to walk and talk at the same time!

John Davis tells us in his book, *Walking,* that walking is "what makes us human. It can tranquilize better than drugs, encourage clear and creative thinking and open up new worlds to explore."

Marge Ferraro, an avid walker, age fifty-five, says,

> All of us should be doing something in order to make the heart do what it's supposed to do. I realized I wasn't getting enough exercise, and we've had family members suffer strokes and heart disease. I wanted to do something toward prevention, if possible. Now I walk three miles a day, five days a week. I've taken off nineteen pounds, I feel much more alive, and I'm much happier with myself.

Walk. You're in good company. Others have walked before you to keep their heads clear and their bodies in shape— Shakespeare, Thoreau, Aristotle, Einstein, Freud, and Lincoln. Take a walk, and you'll be following in the footsteps of a very distinguished crowd.

I believe that walking provides an excellent chance to spend quality time with special people. Each time I see a couple taking an evening stroll, holding hands and obviously enjoying each other, my heart warms. That's nice, I think, not to mention healthy.

Rebounding: The Fun Exercise

Rebounding is one of my favorite forms of exercise. A small trampoline, also called a rebounder, can be used at an office or in the home. It's an excellent option because it doesn't restrict the exerciser due to weather or any other inconveniences. It's also fun, easy, inexpensive, and—most important—effective.

Furthermore, rebounding offers you variety. You can jog, skip rope, dance, bounce, and twist. You can practice your parallel skiing form, do calisthenics or jumping jacks, and, of course, listen to music or watch TV at the same time.

Rebounding improves your overall health and strength at a cellular level because the body resists and adapts to the stress of acceleration as you go up, deceleration as you come down, and gravity. Your cells are cleansed more efficiently because rebounding improves the ability of the lymphatic system to remove toxins and poisons.

Keep in mind that as effective as I've just described it to be, rebounding is only as beneficial as the intensity and duration of your exercise. You decide whether or not you experience aerobic conditioning. I have found that I must be exceptionally disciplined to keep my rebounding intense enough to achieve aerobic conditioning.

These suggestions will help: First, as your strength and endurance improve, begin holding light weights in your hands. Start with one pound or less in each. This will help give your body a better overall workout with emphasis on your upper body. As conditioning improves, graduate to heavier weights, and add a weight belt around your waist and, if you wish, ankle weights.

Next you may want to combine your rebounding with other aerobic exercises. A combination that works well for me is this one: I work out on the rebounder with weights for ten to fifteen minutes, then jog for a couple of miles (or vice versa).

Regardless of whether or not you decide to rebound to achieve aerobic conditioning, it is an excellent form of exercise. It improves the efficiency of your cardiovascular system, your muscular system, and your skeletal system. It improves coordination, agility, rhythm, and balance, with minimal strain on the joints. Dr. Henry Savage says, "Never in my thirty-five years as a practicing physician have I found any exercise method, at any price, that will do more for the physical body than rebound exercise."

Finally, rebounding complements any other form of exercise or sporting activity in which you wish to participate.

The Best Time to Exercise

The activities I've described—and many others, including stair climbing, rope-jumping, running in place, skating, etc.—will give us the benefits of aerobic exercise when done with the correct intensity, duration, and frequency. Remember, for consistent benefits we must be consistent in our investment of time and energy.

Give yourself a regularly-scheduled time to exercise. Then take this appointment at least as seriously as you would a luncheon meeting!

For many, the best time to exercise is the evening because it can complete the body's natural stress cycle. It helps you release and neutralize the tensions of the day and also helps you return to the essential regeneration state of balance, preparing you for peak performance. Aerobic exercise before the evening meal will help suppress the appetite. When you exercise just before eating, you will probably eat less. Keep in mind that evening exercise enthusiasts experience slightly fewer injuries than do the morning exercisers.

If you feel that morning exercise fits with your natural cycle, however, I wouldn't dream of discouraging you. There are advantages to early morning aerobics, as my good friend, Larry J. Payne, will attest. He says that morning exercise stimulates him to face the day with clarity of mind and energy. He also feels that he can create too many excuses to avoid exercise in the evening.

Here's a happy medium—I exercise *lightly* in the morning and save my vigorous workout for the evening. You, however, will be happiest with your own system. Let's face it: Whether you prefer morning, midday, or evening exercise, the best time is whenever you'll do it!

Maintaining Fitness

Today's informed public—especially health professionals who keep up with the literature available in the health field—can no longer ignore the value of exercise. The only time exercise should not be part of one's health care plan is when there is some serious mental or physical dysfunction that will not permit it.

Generally, fitness is lost when you exercise two days or less per week. It is maintained when you exercise three to four days a week. It improves again slightly when you exercise five or six days each week.

To insure proper fitness, you should consider three things:

1. Frequency—three to five times a week
2. Duration—twenty to thirty minutes each session
3. Intensity—stay within your training zone

Remember, before you begin—especially if you are over thirty and/or rather sedentary—begin your exercise program with medical supervision. If you are over forty, and/or are somewhat sedentary, a treadmill stress test is suggested.

Unlocking Your Body's Potential

Let me dispel the myth. I am *not* an exercise fanatic. I am an advocate. Although I do exercise aerobically three to five times a week, I am not in love with exercise. If you think I lay awake nights thinking about my next exercise session, (as my mother used to say) you've got another *think* coming.

I don't necessarily *enjoy* exercising, but I truly do love how healthy I feel and the things I can do as a result of it. Sometimes I enjoy it and sometimes I don't. But I know that exercise is something I *need* to do. It's as essential as eating and sleeping.

The difference in physical capacity between a sedentary twenty-five-year old and a sedentary sixty-five year old is more than 50 percent. But when both are aerobically fit, the difference in physical capacity is reduced to less than 15 percent. Not bad—forty years age difference but a mere 15 percent or less difference in physical capacity. That's why I exercise. The benefits are marvelous. Exercise is the catalyst—the key—that unlocks your body's potential to produce and manage energy and to function at its optimum.

The Presidential Sports Award Program can help motivate a group to become involved in physical activity. The program not only motivates but provides a system of monitoring achievements. An instructor keeps track of miles run, games played, etc. If you would like to start a Presidential Sports Award program in your fitness facility, write to the Council. The logs are free. Just send a self-addressed stamped envelope to Presidential Sports Award, P.O. Box 5214, FDR Post Office, New York, NY 10150-5214.

Whether in a group or on your own, there is no better habit that will affect your health and your overall well-being than regular aerobic exercise. If you are just beginning, start slowly. Soon you'll feel and see that exercise is a living-to-win quality. Your investment will pay off, again and again, year after year.

Now that you've discovered the importance of exercise and some of the most effective ways to become aerobically fit, let's look at several other ways we can learn to change our lifestyle and make living better. In the next few chapters, we will explore how we can feed our minds to improve our emotional health and impact our energy levels.

—Part Three—

Improving the Quality of Life

14

Looking on the Bright Side

Psychologist Alfred Fuller was doing research on the effects of alcoholic parents on children in the home. The family he studied had twin boys.

Their father abused alcohol. By Dr. Fuller's observations, the man was not a good father. Neither was he a good husband to his wife, a good provider, nor a contributor to his community.

Several years later, after they had grown up and left home, the twins were interviewed separately by Dr. Fuller. One had become a good father and husband, was providing for his family, and felt committed to contributing to society. The other had many of the negative traits of his father; he was, in fact, very much like his father. When Dr. Fuller asked each son why he thought he was the way he was, each gave this answer: "Because of my father."

Did the father cause one son to fail and the other to succeed? Certainly not. Each boy's perception and reaction made the difference.

Your Point of View

Decisions involving perceptions occur every day.

One day you come home from work and the kids are running around the house. You think, "Children at play are wonderful." Another day you may arrive home to the same scenario, except this time you are exhausted. Your attitude and energy level are completely different. You're ready to lash out: "How many times have I told you . . .!"

The Greek philosopher Epictetus observed this syndrome nearly two thousand years ago: "People are not disturbed by things . . . but by the views which they take of them."

Events (grizzly bears) have no power in and of themselves. Not even your job, the boss, co-workers, school, traffic jams, your spouse, kids, friends, or pets can cause reactions.

What ignites that complex chain of physical events is our perception. The reaction automatically follows.

Many of life's grizzly bears surprise and threaten us. In the best interest of creativity, health, and productivity, we need to prepare ourselves mentally by managing our attitudes and perceptions. To carry this one step further, we need to avoid all things that hinder us and make responsible use of all things that help us manage our attitudes and perceptions.

How Your Attitude Affects Your Energy Level

Reacting positively to an event is easier when energy levels are high. For example, a high energy reservoir promotes an amiable reaction. A low energy reservoir promotes a hostile reaction.

Attitude is a big determining factor in energy reservoir levels. Negative attitudes support negative emotions, which erode our health faster than poor nutrition. Conversely, positive mental attitudes support positive emotions and health.

Our attitude, then, determines the overall reaction we have to the challenges of life. A positive attitude is the single most powerful quality in determining how you and I handle the multitude of events we encounter each day. Attitude alone can make the difference between coping or collapsing.

A positive attitude is a great quality. It is a most effective vaccine against stress-related disorders and organic disease.

William James, the prominent psychologist, said, "The greatest discovery of my generation is that human beings can alter their lives by altering their attitudes of mind."

Attitude is basic to every aspect of our lives. For example, our attitudes about work affect our performance. Our attitudes toward people affect our relationships. A suspicious attitude will determine that you have a suspicious personality. And a gracious attitude will give you a gracious personality. A person with an optimistic attitude lights up a room when they walk in; a person with a pessimistic attitude lights up a room when they leave.

> A woman hailed a cab. From the minute the driver picked her up, she was rude, abusive, and condescending. At her destination, the cab driver opened her door and helped her out. He got back into the driver's side. Then he rolled down the window and called after her: "Lady, you forgot something."
>
> The woman turned, with a frown, and asked loudly, "Yes, what is it?"
>
> The cab driver gave her a level look. "A positive attitude," he said as he drove away slowly.

How do we go about changing our attitudes and perceptions? It helps to understand how they develop.

What Your Mind Records

All previous experiences and the ways we have interacted with them have helped to create our attitudes.

Our minds function much like complex computers—better, in fact, than complex computers. Using today's microchip technology, a computer with the same mental capacity as your brain would need to be as large as the Empire State Building. Somewhere in the mind is the knowledge and capacity to operate every single cell in the body at every moment in time. We cannot even imagine our capacity.

The brain acts as a recording device that begins the instant it starts functioning and doesn't stop until death. It records on one or a combination of tracks at once. There are tracks to record audio, visual, and emotional sensations. Everything we read, see, or hear, along with any feelings associated with them, are recorded.

As the number of recordings or experiences increases, the tracks begin to overlap, mix with, and override previous recordings. When we consciously or subconsciously tap into our memory banks, what determines, then, which experiences or recordings get played back?

It depends on which program is most dominant. For example, if five recordings in your mental computer say that 2 + 2 = 4, and one that says 2 + 2 = 5, when asked the answer for 2 + 2, it will most likely answer 4.

The second factor involved in recording and playback is the power source, or the energy available to our memory banks. Our energy levels help determine the quality of the recording and the playback. Without constant energy sources, the playback function is unpredictable. Low energy levels make the recordings less reliable. The picture may be fuzzy and distorted.

Energy levels must be maintained so the brain can function at its optimum. Maintaining the body is important so that when we replay experiences the recording will consistently come through loud and clear. But even beyond maintaining the energy levels we can also help make certain that the dominant recordings in our minds are positive ones.

Test Yourself

Let's see how your mind has been conditioned to react to the following situation.

You are driving to work, and traffic is piling up. Your speed is down to ten miles an hour and finally to a complete standstill. You're due at a meeting in fifteen minutes. Recorded in your mental computer are several similar experiences from which you can choose a response.

1. "There's nothing I can do about this, so I'm going to use this slowed traffic to listen to some soothing music or educational tapes."

If this was your response, your bodily reaction to the traffic would most likely be minimal. As you remain neutral emotionally, your body conserves energy. You would arrive at work energetic and prepared.

2. "Why does this *always* happen when I'm on my way to a meeting? This is irritating! I can't be late."

When you choose this response, your blood pressure begins to rise, and a great deal of energy is burned needlessly. You arrive at work harried and hassled.

When you or I do not learn to manage our reactions to life's challenges by managing our attitudes and energy levels positively, we easily fall prey to negative experiences. When we learn to manage our attitudes and our energy, we are better able to respond to situations positively.

Imagine the problems these parents had when they received the following letter from their eighteen-year-old daughter who away from home for the first time.

Dear Mom and Dad,

This letter is to tell you about my first semester in college. It has been both unusual and exciting.

I'm four months pregnant, but don't be alarmed, because Herbert and I will be married by a minister who lives in our commune.

I'm anxious for you to meet Herbert. My only fear is that he will not approve of you because you don't smoke grass or believe in riots—even for good causes like abolishing taxes.

You won't be able to call me because our phone has been disconnected for non-payment. But I promise to write again soon.

Love,

Linda

How would you respond to a letter like that? What kind of attitude would it create?

Two restless and anxious days later, Linda's parents received a second letter.

Dear Mom and Dad,

I hope you didn't lose any sleep over my last letter. I'm not pregnant, there is no Herbert, and I don't smoke grass, live in a commune, or believe in riots. I wrote you that last letter because I got four D's and one F in my grades and I wanted you to see things in their proper perspective.

Very few of life's challenges are as bad as they seem at the time!

Death of a Pessimist

Following is just one example of the power our attitudes have over us.

A man named Jim Bernard accidentally got locked inside a refrigerated railroad car. Realizing he was trapped inside with no warm clothes to protect him, Jim became frantic, scratching and pounding on the door and screaming for help.

Exhausted and shivering, Jim settled into the corner of the car. No human being could survive in those frigid surroundings for long. With a pen he scrawled his last thoughts on the wall: "I am becoming very cold. I do not have long to live. I can tell that death is close. I can feel it very near. These may well be my last words."

Hours later, Jim was found dead.

Rescuers were amazed to discover, however, that the refrigerator unit had not been working for some time. The temperature inside had been fifty-eight degrees, and there had been plenty of oxygen.

Jim didn't die of suffocation, and he didn't freeze to death. He died because his mind had decided that the situation was hopeless.

How dramatically our attitudes and the power of the mind can influence us! Jim's life attitude was probably reflected in the message he scratched on the wall of the unit. His attitude toward life most certainly had been pessimistic.

Would an optimist—one who has a dominantly positive attitude toward life—have responded to the same set of circumstances in a different manner? I think so. He probably would have told himself something like this: "Okay, remain calm. Keep moving to stay warm. Someone will be along soon."

Oscar the Optimist

Twin boys, Peter, the pessimist, and Oscar, the optimist, were being observed to see how they reacted to different circumstances.

Peter was put into a room full of brand new toys. He immediately began to play with them but soon began behaving anxiously. All at once, he began moving the toys, one by one, into the corner. Then he went to the opposite side of the room, sat down, and cried. When questioned about his behavior, Peter said, "I was afraid I might break them."

Oscar was put into a room empty except for a large pile of horse manure and a small shovel. After strolling around the room and humming to himself for a few minutes, Oscar stopped and stared at the manure. Suddenly he became quite excited and started shovelling through the manure. When questioned about his behavior, Oscar said, "With this much manure, there's got to be a pony somewhere, and I want to ride it!"

Take Your Choice

There are times when all the positive thinking in the world won't change an inevitable, undesirable outcome—like the time the window washer's scaffolding broke outside the window of the twenty-sixth floor of a skyscraper. As the man flew by an open window on the ninth floor, he was heard saying to himself, "So far, so good."

The title of a recent article in *Christianity Today* (April 1988) by David G. Meyers and Malcolm A. Jeeves suggests that positive thinking can be carried too far. In the article, "Looking on the Bright Side—Without Blinding Yourself," the authors state that "positive thinking can help us achieve more, but we've got to stay in touch with reality."

Meyers and Jeeves go on to describe some of the possible side effects of an overdose of positive thinking. Finally, the authors concur, "What we therefore need is neither negative or positive thinking, but realistic thinking—thinking characterized by enough pessimism to trigger concern, enough optimism to provide hope."

The true optimist makes the best out of the worst.
The true pessimist makes the worst out of the best.

People tend to excuse themselves from a variety of undesirable personality characteristics with this stock phrase: "That's just the way I am."

But we *choose* the way we will be. Yes, we are products of everything we experience. But we decide how we will react to circumstances.

Shakespeare said, "There is nothing good or bad, but thinking makes it so."

Perhaps in the past we were not fully aware of the choices we were making. But today, now, this very minute, we can begin consciously to censor and choose the input. You and I have the power to make a mental switch—a choice. We do have the ability to accept or reject negative thoughts. We can switch them off like a poor radio or television program. It takes practice, but we can.

It is in our best interests to avoid input that will hinder us and welcome that input that will complement a positive way of life.

Who's Going to Win?

Lincoln had it right: "People are just about as happy as they make up their minds to be." Through positive thoughts, attitudes, and high energy levels, we can keep ourselves from being consumed by negative thoughts.

"I don't know what came over me."

"I just exploded."

These are the kinds of statements people make when they try to explain away their reactions to stressful situations. However, these aren't accurate descriptions of what occurs during stress. Situations don't control people; rather, people *choose* how they will react.

An old Indian commented to his long-time preacher friend, "I have this terrible fight going on inside. It's an ongoing battle between a black dog and a white dog. Sometimes the white dog wins, and sometimes the black dog wins; but I can always tell ahead of time which one's gonna win.''

"How can you tell ahead of time which one will win?'' the preacher wanted to know.

"That's easy,'' replied the wise old Indian. "It depends on which one I feed.''

The thoughts of today directly determine tomorrow's feelings, thoughts, and energy. As we think, so will we feel.

Since our thoughts are directly related to our stress levels and our health, it makes sense to make use of our marvelous mental computers positively. You and I can program our minds to keep our lives in balance and attain what we want most—better health, more energy, or more fulfilling relationships.

Dr. Kenneth Hildebrand has this to say about our human condition:

> In the voyage of life, the waves may pile high, but if we calk the seam of our spirit so that uncertainty and despair don't enter and swamp us from within, we'll reach port somehow. Self-confidence, faith and hope help to keep our ship of personality watertight and seaworthy.
>
> All the waters of anxiety in the world cannot harm us—unless we let them get inside.

Maintaining a Positive Attitude

Let me give you an example of someone who managed to choose positive thought patterns in spite of severe degradation and a life-threatening experience.

During World War II, Dr. Viktor E. Frankl, a Jew, was captured by the Nazis. They took his cap, his shirt, his belt, and his shoes. Then they took his trousers and his underclothing. He was naked. After having a laugh, his captors shaved him of all his hair and took his watch and even his wedding ring. They took everything, looked at him naked, and laughed.

But in his mind, Viktor thought, "There is one thing you have not robbed me of, and *that* you cannot take. You cannot take from me my power and freedom to choose my thoughts and attitudes."

And they never did. Viktor Frankl suffered through years in the concentration camp, but the Nazis could never take from him his power and freedom to choose his attitude. He describes this entire experience in his powerful bestselling book, *Man's Search For Meaning*.

The Secret of Contentment

In order to choose a positive reaction to stressful or difficult times, however, there must be one available to choose. How, then, do we insure this positive choice?

How do you and I keep our personalities, like ships, positive and watertight, so that the negative waters of life do not enter and swamp us from within? The answer lies in learning to control what we feed our minds and where we focus our attention.

The apostle Paul did more than maintain a positive attitude in the midst of trials and tribulations; he learned not to let his circumstances affect the joy he found in the presence of God. Here's how he put it:

> I have learned to be content in whatever circumstances I am. I know how to get along with humble means, and I also know how to live in prosperity; in any and every circumstance I have learned the secret of being filled and going hungry, both of having abundance and suffering need. I can do all things through Him who strengthens me—Philippians 4:11-13.

Earlier in this chapter of Philippians the apostle Paul tells how he is able to maintain this attitude of contentment. He says he *learned* to control his mind. He determined what he was going to think about and what he was going to refuse to dwell on. That's a decision anyone can make and put into practice.

> Whatever is true, whatever is honorable, whatever is right, whatever is pure, whatever is lovely, whatever is of good repute, if there is any excellence and if anything worthy of praise, let your mind dwell on these things. The things you have learned and received and heard and seen in me, practice these things; and the God of peace shall be with you—Philippians 4:8,9.

The secret to true contentment is not learning to control circumstances but learning to control the way you think and focusing on something more positive. My best alternative is focusing on Almighty God, who is *always* more positive and more powerful than the circumstances. When I do that, I always have a bright side to look on.

15

How Emotions Affect Our Health

Emotions can negatively affect our bodies. There is no illness apart from the mind or emotions. Whatever we experience on the emotional level we will experience on the cellular level.

The prolific author and Jesuit priest John Powell noticed it, too. "When I repress my emotions," he wrote, "my stomach keeps score." In other words, what the mind harbors, the body reveals.

A study by the University of Michigan's School of Public Health has confirmed this. The study shows that for those people who have high blood pressure, keeping anger (emotion) inside increases their risk of premature death five times.

Attitudes are experienced on a *thinking* level. Emotions are experienced on a *feeling* level. Emotions *seem* to have more power over us than attitudes. But with training and experience, our attitudes can help us manage our emotions.

Dealing with Negative Feelings

Let's look at an example of how feelings are produced. In this case the feelings being created are negative, and they belong to Margaret Prescott—who has just been jilted by her boyfriend. Margaret realizes that rejection is one of the most devastating experiences a human being can endure. It doesn't feel good.

Margaret's fears have been fed into her mental computer. Her brain responds to the rejection by triggering chemical changes in her body that actually cause her to feel bad physically. Her fears become a self-fulfilling prophecy. What she feared most happened.

Margaret is completely devastated mentally, and her body confirms it. Her mental computer has done exactly what it was told to do. It produces feelings that match her thoughts. But because Margaret is not aware of how her thoughts produced her feelings, she says, "That's just the way I feel. I can't help it." This is a false perception. She *can* help it.

A positive response to the situation would be: "This is really sad and painful, but I'll get over it because my opinion of myself is more valuable than his opinion of me." If Margaret had this perception of the situation, completely different chemically-induced feelings would occur as a result.

Margaret would experience less emotional imbalance, and she'd be better able to handle the emotions she did experience. In addition, she would ward off prolonged or intense and serious behavioral changes such as overeating, fighting with friends, or fleeting thoughts of suicide. Perhaps there would be enough chemical change that Margaret would feel sadness for a time, but she would not experience devastation.

Replacing Negative Emotions

Our minds have the ability to manufacture hundreds of chemicals that can help us feel better. When we replace negative emotions (destructive and illness-promoting) with positive emotions, we produce our own pituitary effect.

An optimal balance is created in our endocrine system, along with the thought "I feel good."

Healthy, well-adjusted people rarely fear rejection. Their opinions of themselves are healthy enough to realize that feelings of rejection do pass. And their confidence in their ability to form new relationships makes the pain of loss a temporary condition.

Depending on the situation—the loss of a loved one, a relationship coming to an end, a lost sale, a promotion awarded to someone else—the intensity and durations of the feelings vary. The need to react positively and manage them, however, remains the same. Regardless of the situation, the healthier you are physically, mentally, and spiritually, the easier and faster you will move beyond it.

Suppose at work you are given an urgent and difficult task to perform on a very tight schedule. You now have a choice.

You could reason, "There's no way I can finish this on time. It could mean my job."

Or, instead, you could reassure yourself in this way: "I usually figure a way to get jobs done. I'll do the best I can."

The first response helps nothing. It merely creates anxiety. The second response produces feelings of relative calm. You accept yourself and your abilities.

It's common to blame situations and others for our feelings. We blame our poor state of mind on the traffic, the weather, our parents, and the boss: "My father gave me a complex"; "She makes me so angry"; or "That really upset me." But we alone have power over our emotions because we choose our thoughts.

This process is not easily managed; I grant that. But we *can* train ourselves through positive and repetitive behavior to become better.

Joan's Complex

Joan, a working mother, felt insecure and unhappy about her body. She called it a complex—a complex that her crass and insensitive husband had given her. He was always making negative comments about her body. She was hurt by his comments and had become self-conscious and quite preoccupied with the way her body looked. One day she described her feelings to her doctor. The doctor was surprised.

"You know, Joan," he said, "for a thirty-nine-year-old woman, you have a remarkable body. With the exception of a few minor stretch marks from your pregnancies, you have the body of a twenty-year-old. Your eating and exercise habits are sure paying off."

Joan began to reconsider her complex. She decided to take up the question with her therapist, who reinforced the doctor's opinion.

"Go home today," she said, "and, in private, look at your body in a full length mirror. Compliment yourself. Do it once a day." She assured Joan that this positive reinforcement would help. Soon her feelings about her body would improve.

At home, Joan waited until she was alone, and then she reluctantly got in front of her mirror and complimented herself. Even though she felt a little awkward at first, she continued regularly for several weeks. Slowly, she began to believe it: "They're right! I do have the body of a twenty-year-old."

After a while, when her husband would make comments about her body, Joan would either ignore them or confront her husband with his insensitivity and remind him that she was content with the body God had given her.

Learning to Disidentify

Nobody can do anything to us that we don't permit. Joan was the actual cause of her feelings of inferiority; she accepted her husband's opinion and reinforced it with negative thoughts of her own.

When Joan changed her thoughts about herself, her insensitive husband could go right on being his obnoxious self; he would not affect her any longer. Once Joan discovered that she could change her feelings about herself, her self-appraisal became stronger than her husband's and, therefore, her dominant mental recording. He didn't change, she did.

The same principles apply to you and me. In order to become more objective about our circumstances, we can learn to *disidentify*, or step aside from them. Anytime we can see options for ourselves, we are no longer victims. Other people will continue to say and do upsetting things. But that doesn't mean we have to become upset or react in a negative manner.

When we disidentify, we keep ourselves from over-identifying to the extent that events or other people control who we are. One of the masters of modern psychology, Dr. Roberto Assagioli, tells us that we are "dominated by everything with which ourselves become identified. And we can dominate and control everything from which we disidentify ourselves. In this principle lies the secret of our enslavement."

The secret to our freedom comes when we can participate in life's events but disidentify ourselves from them. Then we can live consistently in the peaceful eye of the storm.

Why People Commit Suicide

Jewelry salesman Alexander Makowski was devastated. Just three weeks before, in Phoenix, his sample case had been stolen. Now he had returned to the San Diego hotel parking lot to find that his car and jewelry worth $100,000 were missing.

Alexander could take no more. He climbed to the balcony over the hotel atrium lobby, lifted himself over the railing, and plunged five floors. Mr. Makowski ended his life at fifty-nine years.

The real tragedy was that if he had looked in the right place, he would have found his car and the jewelry still waiting for him in the hotel parking lot.

Suicide stories are common. Teenagers alone are responsible for 400,000 attempts at suicide each year. Five thousand succeed. What do these youngsters and people like Alexander Makowski have in common?

They react to circumstances in the way their minds permit them to. Consumed by negative thoughts that produce loneliness, feelings of rejection, revenge, failure, worry, anger, despondency, and depression, they react to life in a way that is consistent with these thoughts. Unable to see any other alternative, people commit suicide out of despair.

But we all have the ability to choose how we will react to a given circumstance. Living or dying, success or failure, and winning or losing are consistently determined by our dominant thoughts and the resultant reactions.

Learning to Overcome Loss

The stress and pain of loss is always particularly hard to handle. Maybe that is due, in part, to our attitude about loss. Our society tends to support the notion that life is supposed to progress along in a forward, upward manner providing us with numerous acquisitions such as friends, loved ones, pleasant experiences, wealth, fame, prestige, knowledge, wisdom, status, power, and material possessions.

The attitudes we carry about life and what we value most determine where we will put our energies. Often what we value most is what we gain at the greatest cost or through the most effort. Conversely, we tend to devalue what is acquired at little or no cost.

This explains to some degree why people are just recently beginning to concern themselves about our environment. It also explains why so many people have such a difficult time accepting Christ's free gift of redemption and forgiveness of sins.

When our attitude toward life includes the belief that people or things are ours to possess and will bring fulfillment, then loss can be devastating. If we invest most of our energies toward something only to lose it involuntarily, we suffer untold pain. This is a natural phenomenon. Our only defense is to examine and adjust our attitudes and resultant actions toward more fulfilling goals and to practice contentment and gratitude for what we have.

When we have attitudes such as, "I must have this job," "I must have a bigger house," "I must have more money," etc., we are setting ourselves up for disappointment and loss with all its attendant grief and misery. One of our greatest virtues is *thankfulness* and one of our greatest sins is *thanklessness.*

When we are not successful at attaining our goals or we experience setbacks and losses, we are convinced that something is terribly wrong. Rather than assess the ultimate value in pursuing certain goals (or our attitude toward the attainment of those goals), we go into a tailspin of destructive emotions resembling a child's temper tantrum.

We must learn to accept the reality of disappointment and loss in life. Yes, we must grieve when we experience loss, but often it is in our darkest grief and despair that we can begin to see ourselves, others, God, and life in a way that will guide us to become what we were created to be.

One Thing You Can Never Lose

Sometime in our life we may hear this bit of wisdom: "You come into this world alone, and you go out alone"—but we really don't want to believe it. The only way to escape this frightening message is to believe that God is there at both our birth and our death.

Only through actually experiencing loss do we have the opportunity to learn how to survive and go on. It is only through the deep agony of loss that we glimpse one of life's most profound truths—that the only thing we can never lose is the love of God.

Romans 8:35 says, "Who shall separate us from the love of Christ? Shall tribulation, or distress, or persecution, or famine, or nakedness, or peril, or sword?"

The answer to this question is found in Matthew 28:20: "And lo, I am with you always, even to the end of the age."

Finally, Hebrews 13:5 leaves no room for discussion: "Keep your lives free from the love of money and be content with what you have, because God has said, "Never will I leave you; never will I forsake you" (NIV).

When we lose, no matter what the loss, the way to survive it is to let go. Let go of the attitude that what we lost belonged to us in the first place. And then take hold of the one thing we will never lose—God.

A Popular Pastime

As we discussed earlier, the feelings or emotions we manufacture are determined by the thoughts on which we dwell. When we saturate our minds with thoughts of resentment, suspicion, jealousy, doubt, fear, and failure, we start the production line moving. We manufacture energy-draining and health-destroying feelings.

Everyone has the power of choice—the power to stop the negative production line by deciding to replace it with positive thoughts and the resultant positive emotions.

Worry is one way we produce negative thoughts and emotions, and we can do without it. Although it is one of the most destructive forms of burning energy, it is one of the most popular pastimes in our society today.

Husband: "You shouldn't worry like that. It doesn't do one bit of good."

Wife: "It does for me! Ninety percent of what I worry about never happens!"

In a study done at Harvard, it was discovered that of all the reasons to worry, 40 percent never occur, 30 percent already occurred in the past, 12 percent are needless, 10 percent are small and petty, and 8 percent are real but divided into two categories—those that can be solved and those that can't.

Centenarians find that one of the secrets to longevity is learning *not* to worry. In preparation for her one-hundredth birthday, Florence McCook wrote a lengthy poem. Following is an excerpt of her advice.

> Never cherish the worries we meet each day,
> For the better you treat them the longer they stay.
> Just pass them by with a laugh or a song,
> And something much better will come along.

Bobby McFerrin's popular song, "Don't Worry, Be Happy," gives us some good advice. He says that we can expect trouble in life, but worrying only makes it worse. If we don't worry, the problem will soon pass. So "Don't Worry, Be Happy."

Breaking the Worry Habit

The Bible condemns worry as sin. When we worry, we are not trusting in God but fearing the outcome of a situation over which we have no control. Jesus said,

> "Do not worry, saying, 'What shall we eat?' or 'What shall we drink?' or 'What shall we wear?' For the pagans run after all these things, and your heavenly Father knows that you need them. But seek first his kingdom and his righteousness, and all these things will be given to you as well. Therefore do not worry about tomorrow, for tomorrow will worry about itself. Each day has enough trouble of its own"—Matthew 6:31-34, NIV.

208 *Creating a Lifestyle You Can Live With*

You and I can break the negative patterns that evoke worry by learning to trust the Lord. Try these suggestions:

1. *Begin a journal.* Concentrate your entries on people and experiences that produce happy thoughts and feelings. You could also include specific answers to prayer.

When you need a pick-me-up or some positive input, review the journal and let yourself feel positive emotions creep back slowly. This practice will help you focus on the positive things and will increase your trust in God. Seeing how He has met your needs in the past will give you courage to face the future.

2. *Don't just sit there. Do something!* Whenever you are having difficulty letting go of your problems and worries, you can keep them from consuming and controlling you by getting busy and doing something to take your mind off them.

You can only hang on to one thought process at a time. So call up a friend, get dressed up, sweep the garage, go out for lunch, play a sport, listen to music, pray, or visit someone who is ill or lonely. Often you'll come back to the worry or problem with a new, optimistic outlook.

3. *Put your thoughts and fears on paper.* You can also stabilize fleeting, worried thoughts by writing them down. With the problem defined, you can begin to deal with it. After writing a problem down, ask yourself, "Is this problem in my control?" Then make a decision. If you can solve the problem, get started. If you can't, turn it over to the Lord in prayer. Ask for God's help in resolving the problem or in giving you the wisdom and peace to deal with it.

The Secret to Peace and Serenity

Let me share a bit of advice with you from Reinhold Niebuhr, who has helped hundreds of thousands of people put their worries into perspective. Taken from a paper he presented in the early 1930s, the following excerpt is commonly called the Serenity Prayer:

> God, grant me the *serenity* to accept the things
> I cannot change, the *courage* to change the things
> I can, and the *wisdom* to know the difference.

In the next chapter we'll look at some ways you can improve the quality of your thought life to help you become the person God wants you to be.

16
Quality Controlled Thinking

Every day you and I are bombarded by sights and sounds from radio, television, newspapers, magazines, and telephones. A continual mental barrage also goes on within us as our imaginations replay past experiences or conjure up new ones. We cannot begin to process it all, and often tensions accumulate.

We need to *reduce the quantity* and *improve the quality* of input. As a result we will be more efficient and productive in our personal, family, and service relationships. By learning to choose what we read, see, and hear, we can program our mental computers to produce attitudes we desire and become the kind of person we want to be.

You and I are a sum total of our interaction with what we are born with and everything experienced to this moment. Granted, the past cannot be changed, but we can reshape our futures. The problem is that most of us are all too content to "let things happen."

Life is a process of becoming. Hopefully, we are becoming what we have chosen to become and even more importantly what God wants us to become.

Who's Programming Your Mind?

Our minds record all kinds of information. Sometimes the information is controlled and deliberately taught.

For instance, little Jimmy Lobash, age five, was pinned under the family's automatic garage door. When Jimmy's older brother, Alan, found him with the breath crushed out of him and no heartbeat, he quickly released the garage door and applied CPR. Jimmy recovered fully because Alan had mentally recorded the method of applying CPR, which he had learned at the YMCA with his parents.

Our minds also record information that we don't control; we don't even realize it's going on. From memory, can you complete these phrases?

Seeing is . . .
One, two . . .
I left my heart in . . .

Depending on your age, of course, you probably had no trouble completing those sentences. You didn't make a decision to memorize those phrases, but they sank in. This kind of inner programming occurs all the time—all day long.

Often that inner programming is extremely negative. If we don't pay attention to what gets recorded, thirty, forty, fifty, or more years of this negative subliminal programming can produce a septic mental climate. It can create an atmosphere in which we are being constantly contaminated.

Improving the Quality of Input

The average mind has a minimum of 10,000 separate thoughts a day. In fact, Dr. Denis Waitley, a recognized national authority on high level performance and personal development, says we talk to ourselves at the rate of 600 to 800 words per minute.

What are we saying to ourselves on a minute-by-minute basis? Most of us do not think about what we think about.

Remember, our mental records play back dominant messages. If 90 percent of our self-talk is negative and only 10 percent positive, the mental playback is sure to be negative.

> A man was pushing a cart in the supermarket containing, among other things, a hysterical baby. As the man proceeded down the aisles, he talked in a soft but firm voice: "Keep calm, Freddy. Don't get excited, Freddy. Don't yell, Freddy."
>
> A lady had been watching with admiration for several minutes and finally said to him, "You certainly are to be commended for your patience in trying to quiet little Freddy."
>
> "Lady," the man declared, "*I'm* Freddy!"

The words we use to talk to ourselves have the power of stimulating and arousing activities associated with them. Words can make active the meanings and ideas they imply.

When you or I decide to control the quality of input into our minds, we will choose words that express the positive because of the likelihood of the corresponding behavior occurring. For instance, you can decide to choose words such as: "I can do all things through Christ who gives me strength"; or "This is the day the Lord has made. I will rejoice and be glad in it"; or "God is love and because God lives in me, I am a loving person."

Another option would be a thought such as this one by Ella Wheeler Wilcox:

> I'm going to be happy today,
> Though the skies are cloudy and grey.
> No matter what comes my way,
> I'm going to be happy today.

By repeating words, phrases, and passages such as these mentally or out loud, the corresponding activity is being reinforced.

To get started, choose a word, phrase, or verse of Scripture that expresses the quality you want to develop. Write it on a card and place it where you will see it often. Place it on your desk at work, by the phone, on the mirror, on the dashboard of your car, etc. Even when you aren't consciously aware of it, that note will be working into your receptive unconsciousness. The effect will be similar to the message you read on a local billboard or street sign.

Controlling Your Imagination

Another area of thinking that needs quality control guidelines is our imagination.

"Imagination . . . ," Einstein wrote, "is the preview of life's coming attractions."

Your imagination can help you visualize yourself as you could be—rather than as you are. If you visualize and act as though you are a loving person, eventually you will become one. If you imagine and act as though you are a gentle person, a friendly person, a better golfer, or an accomplished pianist, and eventually—if you can mentally conceive it and believe it—you can achieve it.

As a boy, Conrad Hilton imagined himself operating a hotel long before he ever bought one. Henry J. Kaiser said that each of his business accomplishments were realized in his imagination long before they ever occurred.

Remember, the human nervous system cannot distinguish between real life experiences and those we clearly visualize or imagine. The body merely responds to what the mind sees—whether the image is placed there through the eyes or by our imagination.

Try this: Visualize a lemon. Imagine yourself slicing it in half and placing a slice in your mouth. Begin chewing on it and feel the juices flow onto your tongue and through your mouth.

Depending upon how clearly you visualized that lemon, your mouth may have watered and begun to pucker. You can almost taste the sour juices. The mind doesn't know the difference, and the body responds as if there were an actual lemon in your mouth.

More Powerful than Willpower

The mind responds to and records a clearly visualized experience in the same manner as it would record an actual event. And just like the audio track, any feelings or emotions associated with the visual are also recorded. When we mentally visualize negative outcomes, we tend to create that outcome in reality. So to use this powerful tool we must visualize and affirm positive outcomes.

In the 1984 Olympics Mary Lou Retton needed a score of 10 to win the gold medal in the vaulting competition. Standing at the end of the runway before her final jump, in total silence and complete concentration, she patiently waited. When she was 100 percent convinced that she could accomplish her goal, she began her athletic and graceful progress down the runway, flew through the air, and completed her goal successfully—a perfect 10, just as she had seen it in her mind.

Learning to control your imagination can cause a natural progressive change that is even more powerful than willpower. Make no mistake about it: When there's a battle between your will and your imagination, imagination always wins. This is why until smokers and alcoholics *see* themselves as nonsmokers or nondrinkers, the constant battle to rally the will is often futile.

Positive results come from seeing ourselves as loving or patient people; from imagining ourselves making wise decisions; and from affirming our ability to be friendly, quit smoking, or lose weight. We can become better

Christians, better managers, better salespeople, better golfers, and better parents. Virtually anything we desire to achieve can be ours—providing we can conceive it and *believe* it.

Keeping Your Goals in Mind

W. Clement Stone, founder and chairman of Combined Insurance Company of America, still habitually spends half an hour each day alone in creative thought focusing on his goals. Lee Iacocca, chairman of the Chrysler Corporation, saw Chrysler as profitable and then helped others believe in his vision, too. You, too, can learn to affect your world in a positive way.

Starting as a one-man business in the late 1960s, Zig Ziglar now heads the Zig Ziglar Corporation, which staffs over sixty employees. They promote, teach, and preach cultivating a positive self-image, setting measurable goals, and developing good attitudes.

In addition to being listed among the Who's Who of U. S. Corporations, his philosophy of "I can" attitudes is taught in over 2,000 school systems. Zig's book, *See You At the Top,* now has over 1,500,000 copies in print. His success stems from asking people to make a "check up from the neck up" to see if prevailing attitudes will help or hinder the achievement of their goals.

Essentially, what we are accomplishing through our mental action steps is placing new and better recordings on the audio, video, and emotional tracks of our personal computers. These positive recordings will assist us in any situation—whether we are facing rush hour traffic, the children, or a speech to a large audience.

Through positive rehearsal you will find your mind telling you, "With God's help, I know I can do this; together we can handle it."

Successful salespeople rehearse their presentations over and over in their minds, along with each situation that might arise. But they visualize a *successful* outcome.

Top executives review their presentations to the Board of Directors in their minds again and again. By the time they actually do the presenting, it's not the first but maybe the fourteenth time they have given it correctly and successfully.

Frank Lloyd Wright, the late world-renowned architect, controlled and mastered his imagination. When clients asked whether their project designs were complete, he replied yes. When they requested to see the plans, he pointed to his head, and said, "The project is complete here. I just haven't had time to put it down on paper yet."

You have mental potential you never dreamed of. You can do things you never thought you could. Only your mind can inhibit you—if you think you can't, you're right. If you think you can—you're right, too!

Mere Human Potential?

For many years I have been a strong advocate of the human potential movement. But I am alarmed that people are beginning to believe that "thinking," "speaking," and "visualizing" offer unlimited power to solve human problems and create health and wealth. Such beliefs lead to the idea that we have the same creative abilities as God and can, in fact, become God-like if only we release enough of our "limitless" human potential.

On the surface this may seem relatively harmless and appear to do a lot of good. But, spiritually, it is playing with fire. I don't want to frighten those who use these techniques honestly in order to improve their ability to function at optimum levels. The danger lies in using them like sorcery or magic to fulfill all desires. We must be careful not to use our imaginations as a tool to gain power or control over other people or situations.

We can use many techniques if our sole purpose is to reach goals or become whatever we want. It's fine to visualize, but it's important that our faith is in God, *not* in the visualization.

God determines what we will have and become, according to His plan. He loves us and wants us to have life and have it abundantly. (See John 10:10.) He suggests, though, that we seek His kingdom first, and then all the things we need will be given to us. (See Matthew 6:33.) Notice, I said *need,* not *want.*

In the apostle Paul's letter to the Colossians, we are instructed on this matter of worldly principles:

> See to it that no one takes you captive through philosophy and empty deception, according to the tradition of men, according to the elementary principles of the world, rather than according to Christ . . . These are matters which have, to be sure, the appearance of wisdom in self-made religion . . . but are of no value against fleshly indulgence—Colossians 2:8,23.

In his fascinating allegory, *The Screwtape Letters*, C. S. Lewis illustrates the way many Christians are lured away from God. Screwtape, a senior devil, is tutoring his young nephew, Wormwood, on how to lure Christians away from their faith in God. Screwtape says to Wormwood,

> Whenever they are attending to the Enemy Himself, we are defeated, but there are ways of preventing them from doing this. The simplest is to turn their gaze away from Him toward themselves. Keep them watching their own minds and trying to produce feelings there by the action of their own wills.

Regarding our self and our mind power, the best philosophy is similar to John the Baptist's: "He must increase, but I must decrease" (John 3:30).

As we seek God's will for our lives, He can create within our own minds and spirits the image of the person He wants us to become.

Renewing Your Mind

It is possible. You *can* be transformed into a more relaxed, creative, healthy, and productive person by the input you allow to enter your mind and heart.

Romans 12:2 sums up the power of quality controlled input: "Do not conform any longer to the pattern of this world, but be transformed by the renewing of your mind" (NIV). Find out what God says about you and begin affirming those thoughts to yourself.

For example, Scripture says, "You have made him [you and me] a little lower than the heavenly beings [God] and crowned him with glory and honor" (Psalm 8:5, NIV). You can say to yourself, "I am created in the image of God, and He has crowned me with glory and honor." Your mind is being renewed each time you understand and believe these truths.

Another verse says that nothing "shall be able to separate us from the love of God, which is in Christ Jesus our Lord" (Romans 8:39). Tell yourself, "*Nothing* can separate me from God's love. God loves *me.*"

There are countless scriptures that can help you see how special you are to God. Each time you review them and believe what they say about you, your outlook on yourself and your world will brighten.

Our dominant thoughts need to be positive and constructive, as they may break into words or actions at any time. Perhaps this prayer will help begin the process: "Lord, let my words be sweet, for I may have to eat them."

Choosing to Think Correctly

Begin now to record thoughts that complement what you want to become and what you want to accomplish. It will take a little planning and a little time, but it can change your life.

You and I are the sum total of our experiences. Everything we ever thought, heard, saw, and felt is recorded in our minds. The audio, visual, and emotional recordings we allow into our personal computers today—and the way we interact with them—will determine who we are five, ten, and twenty years from now.

We can strongly influence what our mental computers feed back to us. We can make choices that will create the kind of person we will become. I personally believe that, second only to prayer, the power of "choice" is the greatest power available to us.

Decide today to improve the quality of your thinking. If you do, you will never be the same again.

17
Giving Your Mind a Break

Our society has become irreversibly noisy. We are rarely blessed with—or allow ourselves the luxury of—relative silence. When was the last time you relaxed by a fire to only the sound of a soft, comforting voice or gentle music?

By incorporating silence and relaxation into your day, you can control your environment and its effect on your life. Learn to spend time alone in restful, natural locations—the park, the mountains, a wooded area. Create a relaxing environment at home. Turn off the TV. Pull the shades. You deserve a break.

Relaxation helps give clarity of mind. It enhances our thinking, planning, creativity, and our ability to make decisions. People who regularly practice relaxation talk of sleeping better and of having more energy and better overall health. They say they've actually watched their performance at work and their sense of well-being improve. They do more in less time and with fewer mistakes.

Taking time to relax gives us a mental break and turns off the harmful bodily effects of stress. It normalizes and tunes our bodies' natural homeostatic or balancing mechanisms.

It is vital to the body's process of adapting and regenerating healthfully.

Walking the Tension Away

Relaxation is the priority pass code into your personal computer data bank. Because tension constricts blood vessels, thus restricting the oxygen-rich blood from feeding the brain, it is much easier to enter or recall data when you are relaxed. Like your muscles, your mind performs best with a combination of activity and relaxation.

Add relaxation to your daily routine. One of the best ways to do this is to *walk*. Not only can it be good exercise, it will remove you from your usual surroundings. You'll have time to think and breathe deeply.

Soren Kierkegaard cited his persuasive viewpoint on walking thus:

> Above all, do not lose your desire to walk; everyday I walk myself into a state of well-being and walk away from every illness. I have walked myself into my best thoughts and I know of no thought so burdensome that one cannot walk away from it.

If we don't responsibly walk away, the following description of modern living could become our epitaph: "a senseless whirl—hurry, worry, and bury."

The Silent Retreat

Few people are as relaxed and balanced as they think they are. I discover this for myself each year when I go on a three-day silent retreat. With a group of fifty to sixty men, I have attended this retreat for ten consecutive years. The rooms are private, and the surroundings are natural, with secluded streams, woods, and a lake. Participants are free to rest, meditate, pray, read—whatever they find most relaxing. The primary rule is "silence."

In those three days I move through a whole cycle of feelings—from elation (at finally having uninterrupted peace and quiet) to withdrawal. Without fail, by the end of three full days there are marvelous and measurable improvements in my overall well being. I am eternally grateful to my good friend Bill Lee for introducing me to a retreat that has consistently renewed me physically, mentally, and spiritually.

This three-day weekend retreat is available approximately forty-seven times a year. More than 3,000 men from all walks of life attend each year. Although the retreat is run by Jesuit priests, it is non-denominational. For more information, write *Director Jesuit Retreat House, 8243 N. Demontreville Trail, Lake Elmo, Minnesota 55042.*

Prayerful Meditation

You can begin to feel the kind of total relaxation I experience at the retreat by taking a few quiet moments every day to commune with God and meditate on His Word. I call this prayerful meditation.

Now I'm not talking about sitting in front of the TV set and reading a Scripture verse during the commercials.

Prayerful meditation produces a sense of peace and well-being that is different from napping or sitting quietly. It quiets the mind and body with no harmful side effects and stimulates conscious, creative awareness.

In addition to the physical and mental benefits, prayer and biblical meditation release us into a oneness with God that allows His peace to saturate our being.

The best way I know to relax is to meditate prayerfully. The Lord instructs His people to meditate on the Word of God "day and night, so that you may be careful to do according to all that is written in it; for then you will make your way prosperous, and then you will have success" (Joshua 1:8).

To meditate means "to contemplate spiritual truths." The Greek word for meditate is *meletao* and literally means "to take care of" or "resolve in the mind." God wants us to consider His Word and "digest" His truth in our hearts and minds. Jesus tells us that the truth "shall make [us] free" (John 8:32). To be free is to be totally at peace and relaxed about who we are and where we're going.

Prayerfully meditating on Scripture has great benefits. Even the psalmist agrees:

> Blessed is the man who does not walk in the counsel of the wicked . . . his delight is in the law of the Lord, and in His law he meditates day and night . . . in whatever he does, he prospers— Psalm 1:1,3.

Practicing the Presence of God

Find a quiet room where you will not be disturbed for twenty to thirty minutes. Open your Bible to a favorite passage—or to some scripture you are currently studying— and read it through one or two times. Begin to meditate on the passage you are considering, and ask the Lord to bring to your mind any special truths He wants to reveal.

To help you relax throughout your meditation, breathe slowly and deeply. This simple but powerful technique will help quiet your mind and body, which will enhance the quality of your meditation.

As God begins to shed light on His Word, thank Him and praise Him. If you become distracted by outside noise or unrelated thoughts, let them pass and begin meditating on your passage again. The important thing is to be open and quiet before God so He can speak to you. Psalm 46:10 says, "Be still, and know that I am God."

During this time the Lord may reveal His heart and mind to you. Sometimes you will seem overwhelmed by the amount of light He sheds on the passage of Scripture before you. Or the Holy Spirit may reveal an area of your life that needs changed. Other times you may not hear anything but have an awareness of God's presence and His love for you.

In our hectic, fast-paced world, we need to discipline ourselves to spend quality time with God if we are to hear Him. Spend time in God's presence daily. The benefits that come from prayerful meditation are cumulative.

Glorifying God or Self?

It must be noted that the goal of many meditation and relaxation techniques is to reach a state of *nothingness,* in which the participant remembers nothing.

I believe this is not only limited in its ability to help a person, but it can be harmful spiritually. Many people while involved in transcendental meditation (TM) and other relaxation techniques move toward glorifying others and especially "self" rather than God.

Prayerful meditation is just the opposite. A person who practices it should expect to come away from each session with a better relationship with God and the world around them. As a result, people who prayerfully meditate regularly feel much more in tune mentally, physically, and spiritually.

Life-Changing Results

My wife Susan has experienced the life-changing effects of prayerful meditation for herself. Here is her testimony:

When I first met my husband, I was a single mother of two children and the vice president of a growing consulting firm. I never had enough time to do everything I felt needed to be done. When I arrived home from work, physically and mentally exhausted, I had another job waiting for me—two children to parent. Often I was harried, overwhelmed, and resentful. Many evenings I was so irritable that I'm sure my children wished I had stayed at the office.

Ron had told me about the benefits of prayerful meditation, but I just didn't have the time! How could I add another commitment to my already bursting agenda? Gradually, though, I began to take half an hour here and there, and I noticed that I seemed to have more energy. My moodiness lessened, too; so I kept at it.

One night, my fourteen-year-old son told me the next door neighbors in our side-by-side duplex wanted to see me. He had a pinched, anxious look on his face. I had just finished my prayerful meditation session, so I calmly went next door.

The neighbors were very serious. They explained that while they had been on vacation someone had broken into their house and stolen some liquor. Since none of the locks had been broken, and they knew that my son's bedroom closet contained an access to their house, they assumed it was obvious who had done it.

I knew that my son would not have done something like that on his own. Little by little the story emerged. The new eighteen-year-old live-in babysitter I had just hired had found out about the liquor and convinced my son to get the liquor for her and her friends.

As I listened, my level-headed response surprised me. I did not strangle my son—I didn't even yell at him, which would have been my usual response—I didn't fire the babysitter (at least not right away). I simply explained to my son the extreme seriousness of his actions and assigned him a consequence. It turned out to be an excellent learning experience for both of us.

I have realized more and more that taking this quiet time is essential for both my family and my health and well-being. Now I consistently take the time for relaxation and prayerful meditation. Because I know how important it is for me, I rarely find that I can't make time for it.

Help for Parents

Both moms and dads need to recognize the vital role relaxation plays in the success of their job as parents. In the book *Parent Burnout* by Dr. Joseph Procaccini and Mark Kiefaber, the authors describe the tragic phenomenon occurring so often today: Parents are too exhausted to perform the task they care most about—parenting.

In his best-selling book, *Parenting Isn't For Cowards,* James Dobson discusses at length the need to maintain a "reserve army" for parenting duties, especially when raising teens. He discusses the typical scenario where a woman decides to go to work after the children start school. (More than 50 percent do!) Then, as her career begins to become demanding and her typical energy reserve has been used up "at the office," she comes home exhausted and totally unprepared for the challenge of the century—her teenager(s). She and her husband now have one more thing in common—exhaustion.

Taking time to relax and meditate on God's Word will replenish your spiritual being and rejuvenate your physical and mental capacities to deal with the complexities of parenting and the other demands of everyday living.

———Part Four———

Pursuing a Balanced Lifestyle

18

How's Your Laugh Life?

Throughout this book, we have been dealing with the *inner* environments—both mental and physical—that help create our way of life. It follows that we should explore the *outer* environments also. These include our activities, the conditions surrounding us, and the way we deal with others. If we understand them, it will help us create healthy environments that also promote personal growth.

I said earlier that the single most important ingredient to health is internal balance. Internal balance and our energy level are determined not only by the way we manage our minds and bodies but also by the way we manage our outer environments.

Yes, the outer environments—including the people who surround us—help determine the overall quality of our lives.

Achieving this precious, high energy, balanced lifestyle isn't easy for most people. But let's look at creating a practical system that will help us do the best we can. The four basic ingredients of the balanced lifestyle consist of play/recreation, work, worship, and love.

From *play* comes joy, creativity, spontaneity, and relaxation.

From *work* comes a sense of purpose and accomplishment.

From *worship* comes faith in a power greater than ourselves.

From *love* comes meaningful relationships and the purpose of life itself.

In this and the next three chapters we will examine the importance of each of these areas and how they influence our feelings and our actions.

People Need Play

When people truly play, they are totally themselves because playing leaves little room for pretense. During play we react naturally because we're caught off guard from our usual overly-structured, carefully-planned activities.

Playtime or recreation time is essential because it gives us the time to withdraw from the demands of everyday routines. We let go of official roles, experience new things, and get to know ourselves.

When we are actually at play, we aren't trying to achieve anything. We give ourselves permission to let go. No longer a means to other people's ends, we exist as people in our own right. It is enough just to be our natural selves. When we learn to play, the other aspects of our lives, including work and family, begin to take on new, healthier perspectives.

Many people, however, retreat to the security of their work rather than confront the insecurities of the world of play. Some hate feeling uncharted, having *unprogrammed* contact with life itself. Leisure calls for independence, initiative, and creativity. This can be uncomfortable for some people. They find it easier to adopt a dull or useless idea of leisure by diverting and stimulating themselves with non-interactive, non-demanding entertainment—television, for example. A friend of mine quipped, "I wonder sometimes if we'd be better off to shoot fewer films and more actors."

There's nothing wrong with some mindless diversion once in awhile. But too much monotony, too much boredom, too much *doing nothing* can produce a sedentary mind and actually cause *dis*tress!

Good, Healthy Fun

Positive recreation, on the other hand, results in *pro*-stress. Constructive play is not a way out of the world but a way into it. It helps us grasp the richness of authentic living. Positive recreational activities broaden our perspective and our viewpoint.

Are you allowing fun, laughter, and meaningful recreational activities into your life? How's the play aspect of your life?

Compare your ability to play today with your knack for fun as a child. Unless your memory misleads you, you'll probably remember a wonderful ability to laugh, enjoy a joke, experiment, and play. When it comes to play, children are experts. Characteristically, they are like butterflies; adults are more like cocoons. We have *unlearned* the art of play. But we can retrain ourselves to be butterflies again.

Let's do a little self-evaluation. What do you like? What's fun? What do you enjoy? What makes you laugh? What ignites your imagination?

It may take some time and experimentation to find out what pastimes are fun and absorbing for you. But once this experimentation begins, you'll be like a kid again. Remember being so involved that your mother had to call several times to get you to stop what you were doing and come to dinner?

Choose a Pastime

Choose a favorite pastime—one that isn't stagnant. Choose one that "re-creates" you by igniting your passion and your imagination. You may be surprised at the possibilities. Stamp collecting, for instance, doesn't sound like a particularly playful activity; but it could lead to a study of government, illustration, history, culture, etc.

Any sport can be the stepping stone to a greater under-standing of the human body, the psychology of mind over matter, and the discipline of practice. Piano-playing can lead to a study of harmony and physics or perhaps to entertaining confined individuals, friends, or neighbors. Gardening can lead us to a study of snails, earthworms, or any of nature's cycles. It can give us a feeling of accomplishment and the pleasant feeling of relaxation.

Play can be childlike. It can magically create in you new curiosity, wonder, and awe. It can teach you all over again what abandonment, joy, delight, and silliness feel like. It can teach you what it feels like to take yourself a little less seriously. Open your eyes, ears, nose, and feelings to the fun and wonders that surround you.

Go Away, Please!

One travel agency pinned this sign to their bulletin board: "Go away, please."

In my contact with overworked executives and workers I've found that everyone needs to "get away" from work. Some companies actually still praise employees who don't take breaks or vacations. Workaholic tendencies in any worker should be a red flag to the employer that this employee may have a problem and is likely less productive than she or he could be.

Take control. Start combatting this destructive syndrome. Try easing into less structured, laid-back times. Prepare yourself to slow down by doing formal relaxation exercises and a lot of casual walking leading up to a relaxed weekend. You'll soon adjust to the slower-paced world of leisure. The effort expended will provide you with the invaluable quality time you need to re-create and rejuvenate.

You may have formed so many negative attitudes toward relaxation that you need to tell yourself:

"It's okay. I can enjoy relaxation because life was meant to be enjoyed."

"I need a break from the routine."

"This day's purpose is for play, relaxation, and enjoyment. I'm not going to let thoughts of work spoil it for me."

We need to retrain ourselves to understand that peacefulness and joy are freely given. All we do is create the proper environment and let the butterfly go.

Are We Having Fun Yet?

Some people merely *spend* their leisure time; others *enjoy* it. Keep in mind that your hobby might be another's work. The sort of recreation you pick isn't as important as the enthusiasm and curiosity that results. A good sign that you have chosen a worthwhile recreation occurs when, although you may thoroughly enjoy your work, you still look forward to your "free time." Play has its own unique release, spontaneity, and creativity.

Another sign of healthy fun will be your unwillingness to stop once you have started. When we have good times, we always have something to look forward to. Rather than running from life, we find ourselves looking ahead, anxiously, for the next surprise, just as we did when we were still in school. Leisure has the power to do that for us. It can be our time of renewal. It can be a time to bring ourselves back into balance—back to homeostasis.

Choose leisure activities that generate enthusiasm, permit you to let go, and produce feelings of self-esteem. They will create an environment that is both nurturing and of interest to you. It will also help develop and maintain your sense of humor, and good humor means good health.

Laugh Your Way to Health

Humor is the most physical of the positive emotions and the best-known antidote for worry. It is a commonly-held truth that it is impossible to laugh genuinely and worry at the same time.

Dr. William Frye said that humor "stirs the insides and gets the endocrine system going—which can be quite beneficial in alleviating disease." When we laugh, positive chemical changes occur internally. Besides making us feel good, these physical and chemical changes stimulate circulation, restore muscle tone, oxygenate the blood, facilitate digestion, relieve headaches, massage the large organs, and restore homeostasis.

Humor heals. One of the most celebrated cases of this actually occurring was reported in an autobiographical book by Norman Cousins, *Anatomy of An Illness*. Cousins had a degenerative disease of the spinal column. Doctors gave him a 500-to-1 chance of survival.

During his stay in the hospital, Cousins noticed that when he and his visitors had some good, bouncing, belly laughter together, he felt much better and was able to rest afterward. Realizing the benefits of laughter, Cousins, in cooperation with his doctors, prescribed several hours of laughter for himself each day. He had movies and books brought into his hospital room: Laurel and Hardy, The Three Stooges, The Marx Brothers, and Allen Funt's "Candid Camera." He created an environment of play and good humor, and he literally re-created himself. He laughed himself back to good health.

Managing Your Sense of Humor

How do you react when others are laughing?

Unfortunately, many of us fear our sense of humor. We are afraid of looking undignified. Frankly, the "wipe that smile off your face" and the "settle down and get serious" attitude has gone a little over b-o-r-e-d.

"Laughter," said the preacher, "is God's gift to mankind." The parishioner added, "And mankind is proof that God has a sense of humor." We can learn to laugh at ourselves and enjoy humor as a natural part of life.

Addison C. Bennet, a senior executive, sums it up in an issue of *Modern Healthcare.*

> Many managers take their job responsibilities seriously, which they should. But they also take themselves too . . . seriously, and that mode of behavior is truly no laughing matter, for it brings neither humility nor humor.

Quite often, the people we admire most are people with a good sense of humor. These are individuals who have *control,* and they manage it without appearing cold, humorless, stuffy, and impersonal.

Humor is an attribute that seems to take people places. An executive search firm in Rosemont, Illinois, informs us that when all other qualifications of applicants are equal, the job nearly always goes to the applicant with the better sense of humor. Other studies have shown that a common characteristic of effective persons in management is their sense of and use of humor.

While studying successful Harvard College graduates in business, Dr. George Valliant found that humor was one of the key mature coping mechanisms—and one reason why the stressful rat race didn't kill more quickly and commonly.

In the workplace, humor allows us a momentary mental break from which we come back to problems with insight. Humor establishes feelings of camaraderie between co-workers, reduces absenteeism, and sets the stage for cooperation rather than unnecessary competition.

Laughter—Internal Jogging

Humor has been scientifically proven to have an impact on several body systems: muscles are activated; the heart rate is increased; and respiration is amplified with an increase in oxygen exchange. All these effects are similar to some of those provided by aerobic exercise. Mirthful laughter is followed by a state of compensatory physical relaxation and diminishing physical tension. It's good for you. Norman Cousins calls laughter "internal jogging."

It's also true that laughter and learning go hand-in-hand. Humor stirs the cerebral neurons. It invites and maximizes the learning process. It inspires creativity. Humor gets you thinking in unexpected associations.

Laughter and a sense of play may be two of the most important interpersonal skills you will learn in order to survive. Humor and play, like any form of nourishment, make human existence possible and enjoyable. It is the one form of exercise recommended that you don't need to warm up to gradually, and you won't need your doctor's approval to get started.

My friend Mike McKinley says,

> Humor has always been a very important part of my life. As I was growing up, I was taught that no matter what, laughter needs to be a part of every-day life. I have always looked for the funny side of things. Laughter has helped me recover from failure, divorce, and life-threatening cancer. If we listen and observe, we can find humor all around

us. My successes have been enhanced and my shortcomings buffered by the always apparent availability of fun and laughter.

Many people say they have a good sense of humor. Perhaps they enjoy laughing, but how often do they let this *funderful* experience occur?

How to Add Humor to Your Life

How do we find our own ways of playing? Start by surrounding yourself with things that encourage humor and laughter. At work or home, be the instigator of humor. Humor tickles the brain, and laughter scratches it. The trick is to be open to spontaneous spurts of the comic in life. It may take practice, but make it part of everyday life.

To begin the process, subscribe to a newsletter or two on humor. This will keep fresh ideas coming your way. I subscribe to: *Orbens Current Comedy,* 700 Orange Street, Wilmington, DE 19801 and *Laughing Matters,* 110 Spring Street, Saratoga Springs, NY 12866.

I can also recommend these books: *World's Greatest Collection of Clean Jokes* by Bob Phillips (published by Harvest House) and *A Time to Laugh* by Don Boys (published by Goodhope Press).

Most of all, take your work seriously, but take yourself with a grain of salt. Ironically, when we take ourselves too seriously, we run a greater risk of appearing as total fools. Business and industry are discovering that humor is not only fun, but it increases motivation, improves morale, encourages productivity, builds relationships, and helps employees cope with stressful situations. It can be "mental floss" that helps clean out some of the accumulated stress of the day.

The following suggestions will add humor in the work place:

1. Make a conscious effort to look and listen for relevant and funny work-related things. Write them down immediately.

2. Organize a comedy or happy hour for your company. Show humorous films to fellow employees during lunch. Establish a laugh library where people can go to relax, read, or listen to humorous materials. Or create a humor hallway. Put up a "bull-etin" board specifically for work-related cartoons, funny signs, anecdotes, sayings, and "ar-tickles." You might even give a prize for the best funny of the week or the month. Here are some examples I've seen:

> A sign in a clothing store read, "Our prices are trivial per suit."
> A sign in the library: "Last of the big lenders."
> A radiator repair shop's advertisement: "A good place to take a leak."
> One plumber's truck bore the slogan, "A straight flush beats a full house."
> And years ago, my creative mother printed this message on the underside of our toilet seat: "We aim to please. You aim, too, please."

3. Use humor in company correspondence. It can help sell ideas and improve recall of ideas or information. Funny can mean money.

4. Make an effort to smile more. Studies have shown that people who smile are better liked. You're never fully dressed without a smile, and smiles rarely go out of style.

5. Focus some of your humor on yourself or a work situation, not other people. The Don Rickles-type humor may play Vegas, but in the workplace it is destructive.

Finally, remember: People who are too busy to laugh are *too* busy.

In the next chapter, we'll take a look at work and see how our attitudes affect our jobs and performance.

19

Putting Work in Its Place

Prior to the stock market crash of 1929, nine of the world's most financially successful people held a meeting. Included were a member of the President's cabinet, the head of an international bank, and presidents of utility companies, steel companies, gas companies, etc.

In the next few years, these people suffered severe financial disasters. As a result, three of the nine committed suicide, three turned to crime, one died in a mental hospital, and the others died bankrupt and destitute.

These people had apparently learned how to make money but not how to make a life. They had not learned the difference between *what* they had and *who* they were.

I'm not making light of financial problems. The most important lesson any of us can learn is not how to make money but how to live productive and satisfied lives. If you truly want to know how wealthy you are, think of what you would have tomorrow if you lost every dollar you have today.

What Money Won't Buy

This poem by the famous *Author Unknown* does an excellent job of putting money into perspective:

> Money will buy . . .
> A bed but not sleep,
> Books but not wisdom,
> Food but not an appetite,
> Finery but not beauty,
> A house but not a home,
> Medicine but not health,
> Amusements but not happiness,
> A ring but not a marriage,
> A crucifix but not a savior,
> A church but not heaven.

As we've heard, *money* isn't the root of all evil, but the *love* of it is. It's kind of funny to think that people will spend money they don't have to buy things they don't need to impress people they don't know!

Christopher J. Hegarty, author of *How To Manage Your Boss,* tells the story of being at lunch with a friend who told him, "Chris, I think you have low self-esteem."

After pausing briefly, Chris retorted, "Low self-esteem? Me? I earn more money than the U.S. President and V.P. put together. I have a home in San Francisco and an apartment in New York. I'm in charge of a large number of people, and I'm considered a leader in my industry. How could you possibly believe I have low self-esteem? You must be joking!"

Chris' friend was now smiling broadly. "You've just removed any doubt I may have had."

Chris says that this incident changed his life. Suddenly he saw how his constant need to prove himself was really just compensation for his faltering self-esteem. He saw how, with every business transaction, he put his worth as a human being on the line.

Are You Over Identifying with Your Career?

Low self-esteem is definitely one of our nation's biggest problems. Little wonder—from birth we're taught that our value comes from what we do and what we have rather than from who we are.

People who are successful have high self-esteem. They are responsible and productive people. Yet they realize that *who* they are is more important than what they do and what they have. People who over-identify with their career achievements can most certainly create a disturbance in their health, happiness, and relationships. Workaholism is as destructive as alcoholism.

Workaholics are the people who assume that everything happens as a result of their efforts. Therefore, they reason, they must always work. They are the people who rarely work a limited number of hours or are always on call for the company. They are the people who think the solution to every problem is to work harder and harder.

Workaholics find it extremely difficult to unhook and let go. The stress they experience accumulates. There is little joy in their work lives anymore; curiosity and excitement are gone; but the addiction remains. There is little if any renewal, and the body never really comes back to homeostasis. The internal barometer slowly shifts until fast forward becomes the accepted norm.

When we keep our internal barometer in balance with the rest of our lives, work can be a source of great pleasure, challenge, and satisfaction. It can add meaning and enjoyment when we know why we do what we do. Working from a sense of purpose is far better than working out of compulsion.

Balanced individuals know what is important, and they know where to draw the line. They can limit their commitments. Their sense of purpose comes from matching their talents and skills and the hours of the day to that which needs to be accomplished.

Working with Joy

In his book, *The Prophet,* Kahlil Gibran said, "Work is love made visible. And if you cannot work with love, but only with distaste, it is better that you should sit at the gate of the temple and take alms of those who work with joy."

It's time we shatter the myth that the measure of our productivity and worth is in the amount of misery, busyness, and frustration we experience. Pleasure and peacefulness are two of nature's indicators of well-being. Acceptance and love come freely with the gift of life. They are not earned by the sweat of our brow.

When we realize that work is just the frosting on the cake, we can keep our self-worth in perspective. We can sort out what is most important, spend our days doing what we most enjoy, and create a work environment that gives to us—just as we give to others. It doesn't matter what you've chosen as your career—whether you're a parent, teacher, secretary, sales rep, executive—the supreme joy of living comes from the services you provide to other people.

Jesus Christ taught often about servanthood. As a matter of fact, in Matthew 23:11 He said, "The greatest among you shall be your servant."

People who strive to dream, visualize, develop, and become all that they can become—and people who help others dream, visualize, develop, and become what they can become—are doing the most important work they can do. They are helping to complete God's work.

A happy, healthy, and productive life is one that allows you to be at peace with who you are, where you are in life, and where you are going.

Organizing Your Work Day

Creating a working environment that nurtures rather than drains is a skill that is developed over time. Each of us must determine the level of stress and the level of pressure that is productive for us; it will be different for everyone.

We've all heard this before, and it's true: The goal is to work smarter rather than harder.

Type "A," fast-forward people rarely have difficulty finding things they are good at. They are multi-talented and work hard. Their problem comes in finding out what they are *best* at, what they enjoy most, and what is most important— and then focusing on it.

Probably the best thing to help us begin this process is to write down work goals and prioritize them into A, B, and C categories. This idea, as with most of the ideas in this book, can be applied to goals at work and at home.

Once you've sorted out your goals, organize your work day so that you can spend your peak hours working on A projects. It can take weeks to do this kind of sorting. In the process you may find that what is important today may be of less importance tomorrow. Therefore, prioritize the activities you want done each day. Do one thing at a time, and delegate tasks that others can do.

Throughout the day, limit your commitments to A projects— the main reasons you agreed to take your job or project in the first place.

15 Suggestions for Managing Your Time

To help yourself further, set some guidelines for yourself and your work environment. Following are some suggestions. (We covered some of these earlier, but, because of their importance, I want to repeat them.)

1. Be cautious about accepting jobs or promotions that take you in any direction in which you are not interested. Chances are these "advances" won't benefit you or the company.

2. Learn to say no *before* you overload. You can't do everything. Responsibly saying no can help reduce the number

of impossible deadlines—self-imposed or otherwise. Remember that your time is more important than money. When you give away your time, you are giving away a part of your life.

3. Be less concerned about how long or hard you work and more concerned about what you get done.

4. Slow your pace of eating, walking, and driving.

5. Give yourself enough time for each task, and avoid scheduling appointments too close.

6. Get away and give yourself a break. Avoid the hurried sandwich at your desk, and reduce substantially your number of working lunches.

7. Avoid taking your work home. It will be there tomorrow. Finish it then.

8. Keep fresh by doing your work in different sequences.

9. Become more flexible. Become less of a perfectionist.

10. Listen more and talk less.

11. Spend more time cultivating relationships with people who have personality styles different from yours. You'll learn something.

12. Get up thirty minutes early to give yourself more quality time to visit with your family and to dress without rushing.

13. Set aside an hour a day to be alone, relax, read, and meditate on God's Word.

14. Harness the miraculous power of filling your mind with positive thoughts and mental images.

15. Finally, incorporate prayer into your work life. Ask for guidance before and during your day.

How to Manage the Grizzly Bears in Your Life

Here's my system for putting external causes of stress in the workplace into perspective. You have five action alternatives that can be used individually or in combination.

1. Responsibly *avoid* the grizzly bears or stressful situations.

2. *Change* them.
3. *Change your attitude* about them.
4. Positively *procrastinate.*
5. *Remove* or *replace* them.

Avoiding Grizzly Bears. At work you may be able to avoid a task that makes you anxious by delegating it to someone who may enjoy it.

During a trying press conference, Henry Ford was asked a series of questions for which he didn't have answers. When it was suggested that this might show a lack of knowledge-ability on his part, Ford nimbly responded: "Obviously I can't answer all of your questions. But in my office, on my desk, I have an intercom with nine buttons. And for any question you ask me, I can push one of those nine buttons and eventually get the answer."

Ford knew the value of delegation. His advisors buoyed him up, offered expertise, and reduced his pressures. He, then, was able to focus on those aspects of the business that used his unique gifts—and which he enjoyed most.

If traffic is a grizzly bear for you, perhaps you can work out a way of reducing your level of anxiety by taking a different route or by planning your day so you avoid the worst jams.

Once you define the grizzly bears in your life you may be able to figure out ways to avoid them.

Changing Grizzly Bears. You know that you do have the power to change situations—and yourself as well. Here's another opportunity. This skill might mean that you change your job definition or your use of time.

Poor use of time is definitely a pressure point for many workers. Because people wrestle with this particular grizzly bear daily, and because it can be a never-ending problem, I strongly recommend taking a time management seminar at least once every two years.

Although we may not be aware of them, there are other environmental grizzlies that can be affecting how we experience our jobs. We can change them.

For example, although we can become insensitive to the grizzly bears of noise and overcrowding, people still need personal/private space. The way your work space is organized may be leaving you agitated, irritated, and annoyed by the end of the day. If so, perhaps that could be changed. By getting into a calm, serene environment periodically, you give your innate regulating system an opportunity to balance itself. It *is* important.

When we feel that the pressures from our work are becoming destructive, our second alternative is to look at the obvious *and* not-so-obvious things we can change and attempt to change them.

Change Your Attitude About Grizzly Bears. Your attitude is more important than you think. Remember that two people working side by side, doing the exact same job, will experience various feelings and thoughts because of their attitudes. Some get irritated standing in line. Others don't.

Perception and reaction make a difference. Don't say, "That's just the way I am." You *can* change—deliberately. It's the inner attitudes that make the difference.

Put Off Grizzly Bears. Learn the fine art of positive procrastination. This allows us time to evaluate problems and decide that perhaps it's not best to make any changes at this time. As was the case in the heavy traffic example, some grizzly bears pass. They are temporary irritations or stress points that can be avoided.

If you clash with a fellow-worker, you can put off conflict. Laying low for awhile, until that person tires of exercising his or her pressure, may be the most positive response to an uncomfortable situation.

Removing Grizzly Bears. Replace the most troublesome pressures, regardless of the instrument of irritation—a new procedure, machine, or job.

Finding yourself in a job that isn't fulfilling or beneficial is a common problem. Relax a minute and put it in perspective. If feelings of insecurity and terror haunt you the instant you consider terminating your own employment, then rationalize.

Studies show that, with few exceptions, uncertainty over job security and the anticipation of leaving a job are actually more stressful than unemployment. Consider this in light of the fact that people commonly change jobs five to eight times in a lifetime. One of the most frightening aspects of leaving a job is the financial insecurity that could result. That's a big grizzly.

Whether or not your work is secure and meaningful right now, you have a lot to offer. Most people underestimate themselves. Because our greatest talents often seem so easy they're effortless, we tend to underestimate their value. So I encourage you to keep expectations high. Then, if you must, you can expect to find another, perhaps even better job or position.

Making a Good Life and a Good Living

If you and I truly desire order in our work lives, it is crucial that we avoid adopting compulsive fast-forward attitudes and self-defeating financial demands. We must also be responsible for consistently putting work and its challenges in perspective, as well as being totally prepared to handle the pressures and the demands it places upon us.

The rewards are great—a living as well as a life. Sensible modifications in attitudes and habits enable people to make a good living and create satisfying lives. Anything else, they reason, simply won't last.

20
Old-Fashioned Faith

We live in a world where constant efforts to improve things make it easy to discard ideas, objects, or practices on the assumption that the *new* way will always be better. In spiritual matters, this is not necessarily the case. My research and personal experience have shown me that some of the old models still work.

For instance, the spiritual principles held by many of our forefathers were, are, and will continue to be sound and effective beliefs. They are beliefs essential to a happy, productive life.

Few Americans today are aware of the supreme importance many of America's founding fathers attached to religion when they constructed a new society that they hoped would give birth to the first free people in history.

You may not know that the settlers at Jamestown erected a cross when they landed. The Pilgrims at Plymouth gave thanks to God for their blessings. Thomas Jefferson referred to God in the Declaration of Independence. And the early Congresses repeatedly called on presidents to declare days of prayer and thanksgiving to God.

In his book, *A Worthy Company,* Dr. M. E. Bradford's penetrating research proves that fifty (and perhaps fifty-two) of the fifty-five framers of the United States' Constitution were Christians—not humanists, deists, or agnostics, but Christians! They were men of The Book who were mindful that those who govern "would be held accountable to a Higher Authority for the use they made of their special powers."

What's Wrong with America Today?

With such noble character and unity in its foundation, why is America experiencing such turmoil today? We suffer from increasing violence, rampant drug addiction, billion-dollar pornography sales, and hideous child abuse. Climbing divorce rates, deteriorating family life, fuzzy or nonexistent moral boundaries, situational ethics, and severe economic quivers indicate that something is seriously amiss.

Senator Jesse Helms asserts,

> There comes a time in the history of all great civilizations when the moral foundations upon which it rests are shaken by some momentous turn of events. That time has come for America. The historical experience of Western man indicates that such upheavals can ultimately destroy a nation— the collapse of Rome being only one of many examples.
>
> Great nations die when they cease to live by the great principles which gave them the vision and strength to rise above tyranny and human degradation.

Such tragic deterioration coincides with the breakdown of the solid religious foundations of our country.

We are in jeopardy from within! Metaphorically speaking, we are victims of an auto-intoxication process. Like the body, a society can poison itself with its own wastes or excesses and leave itself open to infections from the outside. Our social immune system has been severely weakened.

If you are sincerely interested in this great country, the foundation of its humble and miraculous beginning, where it is today, and some possibilities for its future, send for the book *Rebirth of America*. The address is America, P.O. Box 1000, Valley Forge, PA 19482-9990. This excellent book is free.

What Americans Believe

Some argue that America is still the most religious of all countries. A recent survey conducted by *Reader's Digest* and Gallup Polls would *appear* to support this view:

—48 percent of people surveyed believe that religion's influence on American life is increasing. (This figure is three times higher than it was in 1970.)

—51 percent said they are more interested in religion than they were five years ago.

—95 percent believe in God or a universal spirit.

—66 percent believe God watches over them and holds them accountable for their actions.

—87 percent said that they pray sometime during their everyday routine.

—70 percent said that their prayers are answered; they recalled times when prayer had helped cure illness, saved them from harm, and had brought them the jobs, success, and the husband or wife they sought.

—The vast majority said that they are guided by the precepts of the Bible. There were, however, widely differing views on whether or not the Bible should be taken literally.

—63 percent said that their religious beliefs keep them from doing things they know they shouldn't do.

Believing in Anything

One woman, Martha Adams of Hadley, Pennsylvania, explained her religious belief this way: "My religion tells me who I am, where I came from, and what is expected of me."

The results of this poll seem to indicate that an overwhelming majority of people in this country claim to believe in God. The problem arises when we look at the belief next to the actual practice. Even though eight out of ten Americans consider themselves Christians, only 12 percent think of themselves as "highly spiritually committed," and many feel that churches are "spiritually dry."

Another survey conducted by George Gallup, Jr., revealed that America is becoming a nation of godless people with an incredible lack of knowledge about the Bible. The overturning of traditional spiritual values became apparent in the sixties when public demonstrations included signs announcing, "God is Dead."

A little child concluding her prayers said, "And Dear God, I hope You'll also take care of Yourself. If anything should happen to You, we'd be in an awful fix!"

One result of the "awful fix" this little girl described is explained by G. K. Chesterton; he contends the trouble with people who "stop believing in God is not that they thereafter believe in nothing; it is that thereafter they believe in anything."

That "anything" is what I believe the poll is reflecting. Although it indicates a trend back toward religion, many people are *not* returning to the religious roots from which we came; they are looking for a "new and improved model."

Searching for the Quick Fix

Traditional religious restrictions on behavior are considered passe if they produce guilt. We have become a no-fault society.

Many people do not believe in hell. They reject traditional Christianity's concept of judgment in favor of a new "prosperity theology," in which God, like Santa Claus, passes out goodies. We just do our best to be good; and when we mess up, we can comfort ourselves with the thought that we can give it another shot on our next trip.

Many Americans are creating their own brand of eclectic religion by blending the best of the West with a little Eastern reincarnation. Celebrities like Shirley MacLaine are putting a glamorous stamp of approval on the package.

Somehow, worldliness has so infiltrated the realm of spirituality that people are beginning to use religion as a tool to gain happiness, wealth, and security. And not only "yuppie" Americans are doing this.

Speaking from a context of Eastern religion, Mahatma Gandhi pegged human nature when he said that people want "business without morality, pleasure without conscience, politics without principles, science without humanity, wealth without work, and worship without sacrifice." A pill to give Americans a quick fix for their spiritual needs would be a big seller!

In their search for new and better religions, Americans are finding plenty of alternatives to traditional Christianity. Some of the alternatives are: Eastern religions, cults, the occult, and even Satan worship.

Guru-led movements have attracted thousands. The guru's followers relinquish all their material possessions, their families, their jobs, and often their minds to a mere human being whom they feel is closer to God than they can ever get. The Jim Jones tragedy warns us of the potential damage such an individual can do.

Gods of the New Age

People are looking everywhere for answers. The American Astrological Association generates an amazing 160,000 personal horoscopes each year. A direct marketing agency revealed that 7,961,712 Americans purchased charms, voodoo pendants, related paraphernalia, and books and magazines on the occult. These figures represent a 204.8 percent increase over 1980.

Gods of the New Age is an excellent film that explains the alarming facts about these occult religions and their true impact on the people involved. You can get it from most Christian film distributors.

I believe that America has been blessed because of its original loyalty to God and Christian principles. But our nation is turning to other gods. Americans have become worshipers of the creation rather than the Creator. We seem obsessed with materialism and with ourselves. The apostle Paul warns against self-indulgence:

> But realize this, that in the last days difficult times will come. For men will be lovers of self, lovers of money, boastful, arrogant, revilers, disobedient to parents, ungrateful, unholy, unloving, irreconcilable, malicious gossips, without self-control, brutal, haters of good, treacherous, reckless, conceited, lovers of pleasure rather than lovers of God—2 Timothy 3:1-5.

That is precisely the kind of Bible passage that makes people squirm and want to discredit its truth. But stop and think. Do these words apply to the people of America today? Most have become so indoctrinated against anything negative that they would take exception to that passage simply because it isn't positive. Our self-esteem has become sacred. But when does self-esteem become arrogance?

The True Meaning of Success

People with a solid foundation are leery of religions that promise prosperity without accountability or offer situational ethics instead of a strong moral code. They avoid religions whose object of worship is a mere mortal or whose doctrine includes a belief that humans are really gods who simply need to find a way to release their divinity. They understand their own potential, yet they are humble and subordinate to God.

Many successful people recognize that worship has a powerful capacity to make a positive impact on other areas of their lives. These people have strong convictions about their spiritual beliefs. They are committed to Jesus Christ because through Him they receive a clear idea of who they are, where they came from, what is expected of them, and where they are going.

Wallace Johnson, co-founder of Holiday Inns, is an example of such a person. He makes his beliefs quite clear when he says,

> I've had a lot of successes and my share of trials. I've worked long and hard, often as much as 16 hours a day, under some trying circumstances. Through them all, I've learned that the only answer to problems—and to the future of the world—is having a personal relationship with Jesus Christ. The only people who are truly happy are those who have found Jesus.

Finding New Meaning to Life

Julius Erving, better known as Dr. J., the now retired NBA basketball star, describes how he found new meaning to life:

> At age 29, I realized I was looking good on the outside, but was hitting a lot of peaks and valleys on the inside. After searching for the meaning of life for over ten years, I found Jesus Christ. When I gave my life to Jesus Christ, I began to

understand my true purpose for being here. It's not to go through life and experience as many things as you possibly can and then turn to dust and be no more. The purpose of life is to be found through having Christ in your life and understanding what His plan is and following that plan. Now there's no pressure in my life, and I'm never alone. I know that my Christian faith has helped me put my priorities in order. If I put God number one and my family after that, along with my social existence and my job, I can withstand any attack and criticism.

Tom Landry, coach of the Dallas Cowboys, is considered by many to be the dean of NFL coaches. Throughout high school, college, and into the professional ranks, all he thought of was football and winning. Nothing thrilled him more than crossing the goal line for a touchdown—until the day he met Jesus Christ and made him Lord and Savior of his life. Landry is still determined to win, and he still looks forward to victory. But now he says that, with the apostle Paul, "I press on toward the goal for the prize of the upward call of God in Christ Jesus" (Philippians 3:14).

Having that "Something Extra"

The woman I am about to introduce to you is one of the most successful people I know. She is less than five feet tall, weighs less than one hundred pounds, and is in her late-seventies. In 1979 she received the Nobel Peace Prize. She is the founder of Missionaries of Charity. Her name is Mother Teresa, whom many refer to as the living Saint of Calcutta.

In less that forty years, the Missionaries of Charity order has gone from this one woman to approximately 350 missionary homes located throughout seventy-one countries. Through these homes, the devoted workers feed 126,000 families and provide dry rations for another 45,500. They teach 14,000 children in ninety-seven schools and care for 186,000 victims of leprosy in 119 leper centers and another 3,350 patients inside fifteen homes.

When asked how she has done all this, Mother Teresa replied softly, "It is God's work that has done it, not my work, because humanly speaking, it was not possible. He did it. If you do it for Jesus, and if you do it with Jesus, everything is possible to Him."

The Only Way to God?

Many people will not accept that Jesus is the only way. There are many reasons for this. They may feel that other religions provide the same thing. They may rebel at the "exclusiveness" of Christianity and its rejection of other doctrines. They may prefer to keep themselves open to anything that may be of spiritual value. And they may judge Christianity by people who talk the talk but don't walk the walk.

We cannot judge Christianity by the people who claim to follow its precepts. Each of us has free will and the power of choice.

When our world appears to be unjust and cruel, this is the result of the decisions we humans have made on our own, without God. To understand the value and potential of Christianity, one must begin by examining the life and teachings of Jesus Christ.

No Longer a Skeptic

Most skeptics, upon careful study of Christ's life, find that Christianity is not only viable but is based upon historical facts, as well. One of hundreds and hundreds of stories that could be told is that of Lew Wallace. In his excellent booklet, *Jesus and the Intellectual*, Bill Bright reports,

Lew Wallace was a very famous general and literary genius. He and his dear friend Robert Ingersoll, the famous skeptic, covenanted together that they would write a book that would forever destroy the myth of Christianity.

For two years, Mr. Wallace studied in the leading libraries of Europe and America, seeking information which would enable him to write a book which would destroy Christianity. While writing the second chapter of his book, he suddenly found himself on his knees, crying out, "My Lord, and my God."

The evidence for the deity of Christ was overwhelmingly conclusive. Lew Wallace could no longer deny that Jesus Christ was the Son of God. The One whom he had determined to expose as a fraud had captured him and he became a Christian. Later, Lew Wallace wrote *Ben Hur,* one of the greatest novels that has ever been written concerning the time of Christ.

Who is Jesus?

Many people think that Jesus was a great moral teacher or another great prophet, but He did not want to be thought of as either. He made it clear that He wanted people to see Him as the Son of God. When you think about it, anyone who would say the things Jesus said about His identity and His purpose must be either a lunatic, or He must be exactly who He said He was—the Son of God.

The life of Jesus Christ brings forth a very thought-provoking question: How can anyone who led such a humble life still have so dramatic an impact on our world 2000 years after His death—unless, in fact, He is who He said He was?

A brief review of Christ's life tells us that he was born to a poor Jewish couple. Jesus was branded illegitimate because His peasant mother conceived Him before her marriage. His father was a carpenter with no status or influence in the community. The child lived in one of the smallest countries in the world. He grew up in Nazareth, a crossroads of wickedness, crime, and immorality. As a Jew, Jesus was the victim of racial prejudice.

Jesus Christ never married and had no children to carry on His name—a status symbol in those days. He was laughed at, rejected, misquoted, and rebuked by His own people. He was publicly humiliated and then tortured to death like a common criminal. He died at thirty-three, a pauper; His only possession was a robe.

Jesus' ministry lasted only three years. He never got to the metropolitan areas of the day, such as Rome or Athens. In fact, He never traveled more than 200 miles from home. He had no college degree and wrote no books. He had no access to radio or satellite television, and he had no connections in powerful places. At Jesus' death, His organization was made up of eleven men with questionable skills and qualifications. Yet He has more than one *billion* followers today.

An excellent book on the life of Christ is *More Than A Carpenter* by Josh McDowell.

Living to the End

Worship is a personal experience, and who or what we worship determines the kind of person we are. It also determines where we will spend eternity.

I have personally researched and delved into numerous non-Christian doctrines, both eastern and western. Their founders, whether Mohammed, Krishna, Buddha, or any other, fall short of Jesus Christ. Why? Because He is without fault. He is pure and perfect, and there is none higher.

I believe that Jesus Christ is who He said He was, and I include His name in all of my prayers. I am convinced that faith in God and the power of prayer are the most valuable tools available to achieve what people value most: purpose, power, and peace in their lives.

I didn't begin to appreciate life fully until just a few years ago. Today my life has more meaning and purpose, along with more peace and joy, because of my personal relationship with God through Jesus Christ.

The average life span is seventy to seventy-five years. When we take care of ourselves, we can stretch that perhaps ten to twenty years longer. But when you think about it, even one hundred years isn't a long lifetime. No matter how long you live it's got to end sometime.

Life After Death?

I recall what my good friend Zen Ostrom shared with me several years ago. He said, "I've been blessed with a good life. I have a great wife, great children, and work to provide—everything a man could want. And I want it to last as long as it can. But I really get excited when I imagine what it will be like when the good Lord finally calls me home." My sentiments exactly!

Many people hope for something after this life. They ask questions such as, "What happens when I die?" "Is there life after death?" "Where am I going?" and "Is there really a heaven and a hell?" Only through an earnest commitment to seek the truth can we find the answers to these important questions.

In the Gospel of John, the evangelist tells us that God loved the world so much that He gave His one and only Son (3:16). God promises that anyone who believes in His Son, Jesus Christ, will not perish but have eternal life.

My faith in this promise gives me guidance, and it gives me peace about the hereafter. I don't know what the future holds, but I do know Who holds the future. I know that I am going to spend eternity in heaven with my Creator.

God's Way

Most people in America know *about* Christianity, but they do not know *how* to become a Christian (follower of Christ). Many think that attending a church makes them a Christian. But simply attending church doesn't make you a Christian any more than putting your hand in a cookie jar makes you a cookie.

Throughout history people have tried to follow God's laws but have failed because the human spirit is stubborn and rebellious. God's law decrees that the penalty for rebellion and disobedience is separation from God or eternal death. God, being loving and merciful, had a plan to bring humanity back into a right relationship with Him once and for all.

Jesus' life and subsequent death demonstrates that He is the long-awaited Messiah. He is, in fact, God incarnate. By His perfect obedience to God's law, and by paying the penalty for our rebellion through His death, Jesus thereby satisfied the requirement of God's law for all of us. His resurrection proved His divinity and delivered the promise of eternal life to those who believe in Him.

A story I heard recently quite aptly describes what Jesus really did for us.

In the late 1800s, Mr. Thompson had a reputation for being one of the finest teachers in the state of Ohio. Even though he taught students ranging from seven to nineteen years of age in one room, he rarely had any discipline problems because of his loving firmness.

The first lesson Mr. Thompson taught his students each fall was how to behave in school. He asked the class to agree upon some standards to maintain order. His students decided upon five basic rules:

1. No fighting
2. No lying
3. No cheating

4. No disrupting the class
5. No stealing

Mr. Thompson explained that if someone broke a rule there had to be a penalty or the rules wouldn't mean anything. After much discussion, they all agreed that the penalty would be five hard strokes with a spanking switch.

During the first few months of school, everything went along beautifully. Then one day Big Jim came to Mr. Thompson and told him that he could not find his lunch. Big Jim said that he always put it in the same place everyday, so someone must have taken it.

Mr. Thompson had everyone in the class begin searching for Big Jim's lunch. After finding the bag and a few crumbs, they concluded that the lunch had been stolen and eaten. Mr. Thompson solemnly told the class that someone needed to come forward and admit their guilt so they wouldn't break rule number two, no lying, as well.

After several long minutes, Timmy slowly stood up, hung his head, and looked down at the floor. His face became red with shame, and hot tears began to run down his face. "I stole the lunch. My family ran out of food two days ago, and I was hungry," he sobbed.

Mr. Thompson paused for a few moments and said in a sad voice, "When a rule is broken, the penalty has to be taken." He didn't want to switch Timmy, but he couldn't figure a way out of the situation without destroying the order that had been established in the class.

He asked Timmy if he understood the rule and the penalty. Timmy shook his head yes and admitted, "I know I was wrong. I deserve to be switched." He wiped his eyes, turned to Big Jim, and said, "Big Jim, I'm sorry I ate your lunch."

Mr Thompson told Timmy to come up to the front of the class and to take off his coat. As Timmy removed his coat, the class could see his skinny little back through several large holes in his shirt.

As he reached for the switching stick hanging over the blackboard, Mr. Thompson wiped his teary eyes with his other hand. The classroom grew tense as he raised the switch for the first blow. "Stop!" someone shouted from the back of the room.

Big Jim rushed up to the blackboard and with great emotion in his voice said, "A rule has been broken. That's true. And someone has to take the penalty. We all agreed to that. But there is no rule that says I can't take the penalty for Timmy. After all, it was my lunch!" Then Big Jim bent over the desk and said, "Mr. Thompson, I'm ready."

Jesus did for us what Big Jim did for Timmy. He paid the ultimate penalty (death) for our rebellion (sin) against God's laws. The key to becoming a Christian is to recognize our rebellion (sin), and to want to change (repent), and come back to God. Then, we must believe (have faith) that Jesus paid the penalty for us by His death on the cross.

His resurrection proves that He is God's Son and has the authority to pardon us in this way. When we accept this pardon, we not only bridge the great chasm between us and God, we become part of God's family, and we become eligible to inherit His kingdom (eternal life—heaven).

If you feel that what I've been talking about makes sense to you, and if you feel you'd like to accept Jesus Christ as your Savior as I have, and you'd like to have the same God watching over you who watched over the founders of this great country; and most importantly, if you want to be assured of eternal life with your Creator, then sincerely pray this prayer:

> Dear God, I believe Your Son Jesus died for my sins and that You raised Him from the dead.
> Lord Jesus, I accept You as my personal Savior. Please forgive me for my sins, come into my heart, and manage my life from this day forward. In Your special name, I pray. Amen.

Power for Living

Accepting Jesus Christ as your personal Savior is as easy as sincerely praying that prayer. Living the Christian life is a little tougher. To help you begin this walk, I recommend that you read the following verses from the Bible. Please read them in the order listed, starting with the left column.

Romans 3:23	Romans 10:9,10
Luke 18:13	Isaiah 55:7
Luke 13:3	John 3:16
Acts 3:19	Mark 16:16
1 John 1:9	John 1:11,12

I urge you to pray, read the Bible, and attend church regularly—a church that teaches/preaches eternal life through God's only begotten Son Jesus Christ.

For those of you who have put aside the Bible because it is difficult to read, I have good news for you. There are now several excellent, easy-to-understand translations. Two that I recommend are the *New International Version* and the *Everyday Bible* (New Testament). Most Christian bookstores have them or can order them for you.

You may want to seek out a Christian with whom you can discuss your new commitment. I am sure they will also be happy to take you to their church or refer you to one that's convenient for you.

Let God give you the power I've been talking about, not only to live but to live more abundantly. "Yet those who wait for the Lord will gain new strength; they will mount up with wings like eagles, they will run and not get tired, they will walk and not become weary" (Isaiah 40:31).

To help you receive this power, send for the free book, *Power for Living,* Box 1000, South Holland, IL 60473.

My heartfelt prayer for you is from 3 John 2: "Dear friend, I pray that you may enjoy good health and that all may go well with you, even as your soul is getting along well" (NIV). In Jesus' name I pray. Amen.

21

The Power Of Prayer

Prayer is essential to spiritual fulfillment. Faith expressed to God in prayer is the single greatest power available to us. I pray to God every day for guidance in virtually all areas of my life.

In Jeremiah 33:3, God promises, "Call to Me, and I will answer you, and I will tell you great and mighty things, which you do not know."

One of my favorite daily prayers goes like this: "Dear God, Creator of the heavens and this earth, You created me in Your image to know You, to love and praise You, and to serve You. I believe there is something You want me to do today. Please help me do Your will to the best of my ability."

The power of prayer can help our physical, mental, and spiritual well-being. It has been shown, for instance, that a majority of prisoners of war who survived and did not succumb to brainwashing relied on prayer and their faith in God to give them strength.

Dr. Alexis Carrell wrote,

> Prayer is a force as real as terrestrial gravity. As a physician, I have seen people, after all therapy

had failed, lifted out of disease and melancholy by the serene effort of prayer. Only in prayer do we achieve that complete and harmonious assembly of body, mind, and spirit which gives the frail human reed its unshakable strength.

I am convinced that God truly answers prayer. I'd like to share with you about a personal friend who discovered the miraculous power of prayer for herself.

A Modern-Day Miracle

Renee Severson's son was not developing physically as he should have. When David was almost six months old and still couldn't reach for things, roll over, or crawl, she took him to a doctor. The physician found nothing wrong. Renee took the child to another doctor and another. Finally, one physician told her that David was probably brain damaged and would never walk, talk, or lead a normal life.

Renee was devastated. But she believed in the power of prayer and had been praying daily for her son. Now she prayed desperately, day and night.

One day, while Renee was bathing David, she heard a voice in her spirit. It instructed her to exercise David's arms and legs while he was in the water. While Renee exercised David, the voice gave her very specific directions. When she pushed on David's knee, the voice said emphatically, "No! Don't do that. Pull out on his heel instead."

Gradually, over a period of months, with intermittent instructions from the voice, Renee was doing a regular repertoire of exercises with her son. One of the things she did was to hold David by his arms and put his feet over hers as she walked. The voice had said that this would simulate a walking sensation in David's muscles and create the memory of walking in his brain.

When David was about two years old, Renee was finally able to get an appointment at a famous children's hospital in Memphis. The specialists there did an intensive series of tests to determine just what David's physical problems were. The tests revealed a rare form of cerebral palsy, complicated by a blood clot on the brain.

After discovering what good condition the little boy's muscles were in, the doctors wanted to see his physical therapy report. "I don't have one," Renee told them.

The doctors were bewildered. Without physical therapy, they said, David's muscles should have been in a state of severe atrophy. But they weren't.

Renee explained that she had been exercising David and showed them exactly the routine she had been taking her son through daily. As they watched, the doctors were stunned. The exercises were highly sophisticated techniques used by trained professional physical therapists. Rather than recommending that David work with a physical therapist, they suggested that she continue the same exercise program she had been doing.

Without these exercises, David would have missed crucial neuro-muscular development vital to his future motor functions. Now, with continued therapy, he would have a good chance of developing almost normally.

Today, David walks, runs, talks, and functions almost normally. Although he remains slightly retarded due to his blood clot, he has exceptional capabilities in some areas.

Learning How to Pray

God answered Renee's prayers and provided a miracle in the process. But many of us wonder whether our prayers will be answered.

Why God seems to answer some prayers and not others is a mystery. I believe that God always answers us; but He doesn't always answer us when and how we expect Him to. Renee prayed for God to help her and her son. He did. He did not heal David completely, but perhaps the help God gave to Renee served a larger purpose for her and her son than an outright healing.

One noteworthy factor in Renee's story is the way she prayed. She prayed fervently, and she prayed day and night. Persistence in prayer is vital.

Jesus Christ teaches us about prayer in Luke 11:5-8. He uses the illustration of a man who goes to a friend's house at midnight to borrow some bread for unexpected company. The friend will probably tell the man to go away, saying, "It's midnight and everyone is in bed." But Jesus says that if the man continues to knock, his friend will eventually get up and give him what he wants.

So it is with prayer. We must keep asking.

The Lord told another story to illustrate the need for constant prayer. A godless judge was approached several times by a widow claiming to have been hurt by someone. Because of her tenacity, she eventually got the judge to help her. (See Luke 18:1-8.)

The Lord's Prayer

You are probably familiar with the Lord's Prayer. I suggest that you use it as an outline to guide all of your prayers. Larry Lea has written a book called *Could You Not Tarry One Hour?* that emphasizes the value of spending time in prayer. He suggests a way to break down the sections of the Lord's Prayer. This practice will help us elaborate on the needs of others as well as on our own.

Larry Lea makes the important point that unless we spend sufficient time in prayer, we do not have time to present our needs or the needs of others effectively. A 911 type of prayer may be helpful, but prayer is a little like exercise—if you really want results, frequency, intensity, and duration make the difference.

Jesus Christ was often full of tears and agony as He prayed fervently and constantly for Himself and others. Like most other skills we learn, prayer grows more effective with study and practice. We must be willing to *pray* the price.

Ask for Anything—In His Name

One vital aspect of prayer that many people may not know is the use of Jesus' name. In the Old Testament—before the birth of Jesus—people prayed directly to God. But the New Testament tells us that Jesus Christ was sent by God to intercede for us because we had habitually broken divine laws.

The New Testament also tells us that we can have eternal life with God who sent Jesus to stand in for us. Jesus changed forever the way that we relate to God. In John 14:6, Jesus says, "I am the way, and the truth, and the life; no one comes to the Father, but through Me."

This is why Jesus told His disciples that they could ask anything—*anything*—in His name and the Father would do it. (See John 14:12-14). This illustrates the relationship that Jesus Christ has with God the Father. When we pray to God in Jesus' name, we are using God's chosen intermediary.

Another way to explain Jesus' role is to say that He "sponsors" our entry into God's family. Most people are familiar with organizations, clubs, and associations that require new applicants to have a sponsor in order to join. God's family is similar—with one big difference. In human associations, any member can sponsor you. In God's family, only the Lord Jesus Christ can sponsor you.

My wife, Susan, and I begin each day by praying for God's guidance in our lives and in the lives of others. Throughout the day, I turn to God in worship and in prayer for continued support and guidance. With my family, I begin each prayer with thanks for the many gifts and blessings God has given us; and we end with Jesus' name.

I've heard it said, "Pray as if everything depends on God, and work as if everything depends on you." Amen to that.

22

Living and Loving

We all need people who will love and support us. Dr. Viktor E. Frankl, author of the best seller, *Man's Search For Meaning,* wrote,

> A key to maintaining good health is being able to get emotional support from other people. You have to have good relations with your intimates. There are cases on record of people who were called hopeless, but they pulled through because of their belief not only in themselves, but in the people who were aiding them.

Love can prevent or correct physical ailments. Physicians prove this in study after study. Cancer victims, for instance, who have survived for long periods of time were consistently vigorous, assertive, optimistic, and had a history of constructive social relationships. Among pregnant women, complications are nearly three times less likely in a high support group than in a low support group.

Support systems have been shown to reduce the amount of medication required and change the biochemistry of the immune system. On the other hand, those who feel abandoned and rejected often have to fight for their lives. Divorced individuals have twelve times the chance of contracting an illness during the year following a divorce than they normally would.

By realizing the value of positive personal relationships, we can come closer to controlling our health by involving ourselves with vital support networks.

The Love Network

You can create your own resource pool of people who provide friendship, security, trust, feedback, and counsel. Let's call it a love network.

The kind of love I'm talking about is God's kind of love—the Greeks call it *agape*. Agape love means to choose another person's highest good above your own. Another term for it is *selfless benevolence*.

When Jesus Christ suffered and died on the cross for the sins of the world, He was performing the greatest act of agape love ever known. And this is what He asks of us. We must reach out to love and help other people who need us—even we when don't *feel* like it or when it is inconvenient.

Here's how one author describes love:

> By it we are born, through it we are sustained, and for it, we will sacrifice life itself. Love insulates the child, gives joy to you, and comfort and sustenance to the aging. Love cures the sick, raises the fallen, comforts the tormented, inspires the composer, the novelist, the painter, and the poet—Anthony Walsh.

Our support systems begin through our willingness to come together and help make each other feel worthwhile. They are non-possessive and non-threatening. When careers or relationships are changing, they offer us stability in unstable times.

Both your self-image and your self-esteem are influenced by the kind of support systems you have at work, home, play, and worship. *Self-image* is how you see yourself. *Self-esteem* is how you feel about yourself.

Consider whether you're surrounding yourself with people who increase your confidence and acceptance of yourself. Are they people who enhance your daily performance? People who help create an environment for growth? Who help you gain new interests and competencies? Who assist you in reaching your goals? Are the people in your life improving or at least complementing your physical and psychological health?

Choosing the People on Your Team

Support systems are precious commodities. It is ironic, then, that most of us let our love networks evolve by accident. We tend to spend time with whoever happens to be around. We allow ourselves to be manipulated by our circumstances. Our people networks often become sources of distress and aggravation rather than sources of help and comfort.

When we spend time with people who are always crying the blues, it's easy to get dragged into the pit with them. As your outlook on life turns sour, your energy begins to drain. On the other hand, when you spend time with optimistic types, you feel the positive effects of that brightness creeping in. And believe me, association with the optimist cools the affection for the pessimist.

You *can* choose your friends.

People with good support networks surround themselves with caring people. They work at it. The people they select help them accomplish those things they most want to accomplish. We are born with our relatives, but we can choose our friends.

The most concise description of a support system's value comes from my good friend Bill Rezmerski. He uses an acronym— T.E.A.M.: Together Everyone Achieves More.

The people in your resource pool may or may not be aware that they are part of your team, but you will still feel their strength and support. And in order for it to be a mutually satisfying relationship, they will sense the same from you. Together you will be less vulnerable to the challenges and stresses of life.

Your support system can be formally organized, as in support groups. Or it can consist of family, friends, co-workers, or relatives.

Building an Extended Family

It used to be true that people could rely on that natural network of aunts, uncles, cousins, grandparents, etc. to support them. In our twentieth-century situation, however, it's up to us to create our own extended families. This is essential.

The ongoing, purposeful pursuit of healthy, supportive, and loving relationships clearly helps to produce a stable and healthy environment. Since these relationships can reduce our vulnerability to unstable conditions—and even prevent them from occurring—they make it safer for us to grow and develop.

The support of others can strongly influence the changing of bad habits and provide the beginning for good ones. That's why dieting together, jogging together, talking together, studying together, etc. are all such effective methods of improving anything that could be done alone.

> Love alone is capable of uniting living beings in such a way as to complete and fulfill them. For love alone takes them and joins them by what is deepest within themselves . . . Someday, after we

have mastered the winds, the waves, the tides, and gravity, we shall harness for God the energies of love. Then, for the second time in the history of the world, we will have discovered fire—Teilhard de Chardin.

Learning to Love

We can learn to love. Bell Telephone's "reach out and touch someone" is a powerfully moving idea, in addition to being effective advertising. Regardless of your age, you can become better at love. Your only investment is the risk of intimacy and reaching out.

The first thing we can do to improve our present support networks is accept the fact that they can be improved.

Several months ago, the Sunday sermon focused on the importance of expressing love to others. To get us started, our pastor asked us to turn to the person sitting next to us and say "I love you."

The person next to me was a dignified looking elderly lady. After a brief pause, she said with a smile, "Wanna just be friends?"

We don't often think of love—the purest form of support—as something we learn, but it is. One of the many exciting aspects of our potential is our ability to learn, unlearn, and relearn. Regardless of your age, you can become better at loving.

I'm not underestimating that risk. It's a great one, but the alternative is loneliness (one of the major sources of mental discomfort and stress). Love will give you the freedom to grow and become what you can. In turn, you will have something to give and share with others.

As best-selling author and teacher Leo Buscaglia says, "Your greatest statement of love is being able to say, 'I am becoming, not only for me, but for everyone.'"

If you don't give love away, you don't have it. You experience love to the extent that you give it away. You can fill your days with nurturing, supporting, and loving relationships that add fulfillment to your life.

Your Family Unit

Today you'll find almost everything in the average American home—except the family!

One of the greatest tragedies in our society has been the breakdown of the family as a unit. Let's not forget to include in our support networks those people right under our own roofs—spouses, children, parents, etc.

I asked an old friend of mine the secret of his very successful fifty-year marriage. He paused a few moments and then responded, "Virtually since our marriage began, we've made a date twice a week—candlelight, soft music, dinner, and casual conversation. She goes on Mondays; I go on Fridays!"

Unfortunately, studies show that the average married couple—after the first year of marriage—spends an estimated thirty-seven minutes a week talking together about issues or feelings more important than the weather or whether or not the lawn needs mowing.

I made this dramatic statement to the participants in a seminar I was conducting recently, and from the back of the room came, "*That* much?"

The problem spreads into parent-child relationships, too, with the average parent spending only three to five minutes each day talking with their children about things other than "carry out the garbage, clean up your room, and be home by ten or else." Remember, children are natural mimics.

One of the cutest stories I've ever heard that illustrates the impact of adult behavior on our children takes place in a drug store. A mother and her six-year-old daughter came to the checkout counter. While ringing up the items, the druggist was charmed by the little girl. Showing a soft spot for her, he gave her a big piece of candy. The mother prompted her daughter with, "Well, what do you say, Julie?" After a brief pause, Julie smiled at the druggist and said, "Charge it."

Yes, children act like their parents in spite of attempts to teach them otherwise.

Love is Something You Do

With both spouses and children, quality communication time is important if we are to build strong, supportive, and meaningful relationships. The lack of time and the breakdown of communication in marriages and families is a common cause of pressures and stress that can accumulate to extremely volatile levels.

Consistently, the best times for quality communication to take place are in the evening prior to sleep and in the morning before we get involved in the activities of the day. These are the times when children of *all ages* are most receptive. A few minutes spent constructively during these times can be more valuable than an hour during the more active times of the day.

A wife, somewhat pleading and somewhat complaining, said to her husband, "We've been married twenty-five years, and the last time I remember you telling me you love me was on our wedding night."

"Don't worry," he replied, "if it changes I'll let you know."

We need to tell our spouses, family, and friends that we love them with our words and by our actions. When we tell someone we love them and why, the feelings that result are not only positive and pleasant, they are health-promoting.

Praise is the steam that rises from a warm heart. Many people deserve our vocal gratitude—the child mowing the lawn, the loved one wearing something special, the co-worker who passes an article of interest our way, and so on. More than a feeling, love is an expression and an action—it is our behavior.

Where We Learn to Love

The family is where we *learn* how to behave in relationship to others, how to develop relationships with others, and how to love and support each other. Dr. D. James Kennedy in his book, *Learning to Live with the People You Love* says, "God placed us in families so we can discover in our earthly relationships something of that special treasure found only in heaven above."

The love and support we derive from the family unit is the bedrock of this great country. The health and longevity of our nation depend upon this premise.

Because of the importance of this foundation, I'd like to encourage you to take a long and honest look at *your* family life, *your* support system. If it's not what you think it should be, look to other resources such as your spouse, other couples, books, and professional counseling.

Remember, we are not born with our parenting, marriage, and family relationship skills, *we learn them*.

A Family in Crisis

Sometimes we learn about love through desperate situations. Take David McNally, for instance.

He, his pregnant wife, Jo, and their four children left Australia to relocate in the United States. After four years of negotiation, an American company had finally persuaded David to join its staff.

But within four months, the company was sold, and the new owners were not prepared to give David the same considerations. He quit. The next few months were miserable, but David became inspired by the story of Terry Fox, the young boy who ran across Canada on one leg to raise money for cancer research.

He determined to produce a film about Terry Fox that could serve as a unique motivational tool for others. The obstacles were overwhelming, but this resistance only served to make David more determined to complete the project. His preoccupation pushed him and his family to the brink of emotional and financial bankruptcy. David and Jo separated, and his family returned to Australia.

As David remembers it, the next few months were full of introspection and unbearable pain. Finally, in desperation, he reached out and asked for help.

David realized how much he needed the love and support of others—especially his family. He says, "When I shared my pain, when I became vulnerable, I found that others really cared. They reached out and loved me." David traveled to Australia to reconcile with his wife and family.

Reunited, the family returned to America. The film about Terry Fox called *The Power of Purpose* was completed. Today David continues to set goals for his life, but he consistently works at keeping a balance in his life. Daily, he invests an average of one hour reading, reflecting, and praying. David now feels that we are all looking to be loved.

How to Build Positive Relationship

Dale Carnegie once commented, "You can make more friends in two months by becoming interested in other people than you can in two years by trying to get people interested in you."

First, actively and deliberately cultivate relationships. Seek out groups or organizations who share your particular needs, you beliefs, your goals, your interests, or your concern for a particular issue.

People want to belong. The closer the bonds, the stronger the community and the deeper the roots grow in relationships. The need to belong generally cuts across socioeconomic status, education, and age. Most often we will find that people who appear to be "different" are, underneath, much like us.

The local church provides the most well-rounded system of support. There you will be surrounded by spiritually-minded people who are trying to live by the principles of God's Word. Their love and encouragement are priceless in a day and age when commitment and sacrifice are sorely lacking.

Within the local church are many types of support groups, from prayer chains to home fellowships. But it's up to you to become involved in areas of ministry or activity that will meet your needs and the needs of others.

Begin creating positive relationships by developing faith and trust in others. These are two important ingredients in establishing long-term, meaningful relationships. Together they provide the perfect bridge between you and your family, children, and friends.

Once you accept these basic premises of supportive relationships, you can meet new people, call up a friend when you're down, reach out to your spouse (even though it means taking risks), and give support, realizing that is is one of the best ways to *receive* it.

Dependence or Independence?

Perhaps I should add one word of caution regarding support groups. They are not a panacea. We can't allow ourselves to slip into a romantic notion that other people and other things can heal all.

If we look at friendships as the cure-all that will fulfill our deepest needs, we may very well find ourselves sorely disappointed. When we look to friends to take away our deepest pain, we are expecting something that another person cannot give.

No other human being can completely understand you; no human being is capable of giving you total, unconditional love; no human being can offer constant affection; and no human being is able to enter into the core of your being and heal your broken heart.

Only Jesus Christ can do all of the above all of the time. But He often uses other people to help meet our needs. Since we can never stand completely alone, perhaps we can learn to lean lightly on one another.

Now that we realize that other people cannot possibly satisfy *every* need, we can't use this knowledge as an excuse never to risk intimacy at all. Either extreme, whether dependence or independence, must be avoided.

Developing meaningful, supportive relationships, whether with another person, group, or organization will stimulate us in positive and healthy ways. Caring, sharing, and supportive environments clearly help create emotionally healthier individuals who become more resistent and resilient to the disease and stress-related disorders of our time.

Man's Best Friend

Animals can also enhance our support network. Pets have an innate ability to be loyal, unquestioning friends and help create feelings of acceptance. The fact is often validated in nursing homes. In cases where very ill people received a pet, the involved elderly person usually feels a lifting of loneliness and a faster recovery.

Children who take responsibility for pets often learn about meaningful relationships. Take the violent, street-smart eleven-year-old studied by Dr. Boris M. Levinson, professor at Yeshiva University. This child didn't even know what a rabbit *looked* like when he arrived at a rural rehabilitation center. The center's 4-H chapter introduced him to his own angora rabbit. During the course of his treatment, he raised and cared for his pet—and changed into a communicating, responsive child.

Animals are nonjudgmental. Dogs don't demand conformity; cats don't demand change; and parakeets chatter in spite of their owner's irritating quirks, appearance, or personality. History is full of stories of pets helping people through major crises. Prisoners of war have been known to make pets of mice and even insects. The Birdman of Alcatraz is a well-known example.

What Goes Around Comes Around

Martin Luther King, Sr. died in 1984. During his life, he saw his wife and famous son shot down. Another of his sons drowned. Yet, this preacher's message remained one of love and forgiveness: "I speak to my people about what it means to love. We have to rid ourselves of every ounce of hate. We cannot afford it. I know what that leads to."

Jesus said that the second most important commandment after loving God was that we love one another. Love holds not only relationships but whole civilizations together. Love is the life source, the energy of your spirit.

"It is this intangible thing, love," said Karl Menninger, "love in many forms, which enters into every therapeutic relationship. It is an element which finds and heals, which comforts and restores, which works what we have to call for now—miracles."

Most look for love in others and in things. Love does not come from the outside in. It comes from being one's true self—from the inside out. It is a power as well as a process, the only sanity. A world in love is a world at peace. I believe that our true purpose is to learn to love, and the only way to receive love is to love. And let's not forget that we are fashioned and shaped by what we love.

What you give out comes back.

A young boy, having been strongly disciplined by his father, shouted, "I hate you!" and ran outside.

He ran to a nearby hill. In his anger he yelled out again, "I hate you! I hate you!"

He was startled when a voice answered back,

"I hate you! I hate you!" It frightened him, and he dashed back into the house.

"Dad," he cried, "There's a mean person outside who said, 'I hate you!' Did you hear him?"

"Yes," the father answered. "I did." He led the boy back out to the hill. "Call out again," he instructed, "but this time say, 'I love you.' "

"I love you!" yelled the boy. "I love you!"

The mysterious voice echoed back faintly: "I love you, I love you."

"That's the way life is, Son. What you give life, it will return to you. Treat others the way you'd like to be treated."

Taking the Risk

So many times we have pre-conceived notions of what relationships are supposed to be like. We expect to give and receive love in a packaged format with identifiable characteristics. But we must risk giving love, talking about love, touching with love, and not putting boundaries on any of our loving expressions to others. Only then will we begin to see a glimpse of what love is truly like.

When you combine the qualities of a balanced play, work, worship, and love life, you are helping to create a dynamic synergism that gives you the healthy and highly desired winner's edge. Creating a new and better lifestyle means you can really live to your fullest potential.

23

It's Up to You

Several months ago, we had some friends over for brunch after church. One of our friends commented, "The Lord sure has blessed you with a wonderful home!" I had heard that before, but, for some reason, I paused and then replied, "Yes, but you should have seen it when He had it all to Himself."

The house had been vacant for two years before we moved in and was in dire need of a lot of elbow grease and tender loving care. We provided that.

God gave us a house with the potential to be a wonderful home. Just as our homes are in need of care and attention to keep them functioning and to bring out their fullest potential, we also need care and attention to keep functioning and to realize our fullest God-given potential.

This reminds me of a bumper sticker I've seen that said, "Be patient, God isn't finished with me yet." Well, He isn't finished with *me* yet; how about you?

The Domino Effect

When you improve your mind, your body, or your environment, you create a cause-and-effect chain reaction that changes your whole life. When one of the major divisions in your life changes, so do the other two. It's like a circle made up of dominoes. Tip one over—start at any section of the circle—and the others follow. Or touch one part of a hanging mobile; the whole mobile begins to move.

Begin one good habit and observe how it affects the other areas of your life. Begin exercising regularly, for example, and see how you will begin to manage your fast forward attitudes and the stress that's been plaguing you.

That's the good thing about the three major areas we have discussed—they are interdependent.

Perhaps this renewal of attitude and body will help reduce your cravings for cigarettes, which will reduce your blood pressure, positively affect your diet and your weight, and contribute to high energy. Overall, your attitude and your health will be much better. Any positive changes you make will probably contribute to your potential for play, work, worship, and love.

Enter the circle at any point—mind, body, or environment—and your efforts will have an immediate affect on the other areas of your life. Better yet, enter in and make improvements in *each* of the three areas, and you are sure to send the energy-draining and health-destroying dominoes tumbling. Each time you complete one of the action steps suggested in this book, you are investing in your God-given potential—your bright and exciting future.

Raising Your Energy Level

The better your physical condition, your mental attitudes, and your environment, the more efficiently you are able to manage the ever-demanding energy requirements of the world you live in. The energy we need as participating members in a highly pressured, active lifestyle is *not* a given. It comes from within, from what I call the *adaptive energy reservoir.*

When we maintain a high energy reservoir, we are better prepared and better able to adapt efficiently to the demands of the day with energy to spare. Your reserve will help you handle unexpected pressures.

Think of the reservoir as a battery. As demands increase, the battery releases more and more energy. It also tends to weaken. Your energy level drops, and your adaptive powers decrease. When this drain continues over prolonged periods of time, you become more susceptible to physical and behavioral changes.

The resulting physical changes can be as mild as muscle tension or as severe as a heart attack. Behavioral changes can be as mild as a rise in the volume and tension in your voice or as tragic as depression resulting in suicide.

But the premise I'm offering, the bright ray of hope, is that whether a problem is physical, mental, or environmental, you and I can deal with it efficiently when our energy reservoirs are full.

How to Avoid Burnout

Exhaustion can be disabling. Whether it's a long or short-term condition, the popular word used to describe it is "burnout." The best definition I have ever heard of the malady is "too much giving and not enough taking care of oneself."

A dead battery and burnout are both results of too much energy going out and not enough coming in. You wouldn't expect your car or your lawn mower to run twenty-four hours a day for sixty, seventy, eighty, or more years without proper fuel and responsible maintenance.

The biological human machine operates twenty-four hours a day, seven days a week. Your only responsibility toward this amazing machine is that you put in as much as you take out.

The whole concept of this book is about taking care of yourself and insuring that enough energy is generated and available when you need it. Your generator, your ability to recharge, lies within.

You can begin the process merely by deciding to do so. You've been preparing the soil. You've planted the seeds. Your choices and decisions will produce your physical and emotional make-up ten, twenty, and thirty years from now.

Through the thoughts you *let* yourself think, through the physical condition you are developing, and through the environment you are creating, you are choosing how well you take care of yourself—and how well you are prepared to go the distance and enjoy it.

Keeping Your Body in Business

Taking care of your energy reserves is much like taking care of a business. You are chairman of the board. You are also the board of directors, the president, the vice president, and the employees. Your only product is energy, which is produced in-house. You are open for business *all of the time.*

You have three customers: the mind, the body, and the environment. All three are related and interdependent. They are excellent customers but very demanding.

You seldom know, for instance, when an order will be placed or how large an order it will be. Frequently, one or more of these customers will want an order filled *immediately.* It is therefore essential that you have enough quality inventory on hand to fill these erratic and unpredictable demands.

How do you accomplish all that's expected of you? How do you run a smooth shop? Here are a couple of suggestions that will help you begin:

1. Consistently evaluate how cost effective and efficient your energy production is.
2. Keep a perpetual product inventory. Just how much energy reserve do you have—right now?

I know this is easier said than done. To keep track, use a checklist. It will provide you with the guidelines and the direction for a dynamic, healthy, and successful business.

Your checklist is based on the common qualities, habits, and lifestyle characteristics of people who consistently experience a high level of energy and health. These people are responsible, contributive, and successful. They are preparing to win, regardless of their circumstances. Their quality of life is excellent.

Like them, you can create a healthy lifestyle by enrolling in the "Whole Person Health Insurance Policy" and keeping your premium paid. (I have provided a copy of this policy for you at the end of this chapter.)

Moving Beyond Just Living

Are you and I doing the best we can? Each day, based on this policy, you can write yourself a prescription that better prepares you to meet life's challenges, as well as to enjoy life's pleasures more fully. The greater the number of these lifestyle premiums you are able to check *positively* each day, the more you help create that powerfully synergistic and healthy environment needed to run your personal business of producing and managing energy successfully.

The major difference between those who put up with an unhealthy lifestyle and those who are creating a lifestyle they can live with is the way in which they care for themselves. High achievers consistently put their knowledge of self-care into disciplined action. Low achievers do not.

I hope you are seeing that the choices we make give us more control, capabilities, and potential.

Keep in mind that you won't be alone in your efforts to add positive changes to your life. Here's what one person told me:

> My time is split between managing a small over-worked staff and delivering many programs. I

292 *Creating a Lifestyle You Can Live With*

have, at times, felt pulled in many different directions. A lot of people have tried to direct or influence my priorities. This all translates into conflicting pressures and long hours. To deal with these pressures and to minimize my health risks more effectively, I have increased the ways I take care of myself.

A friend of mine uses the phrase, "healthy self-ishness," and that seems to set the tone for me. I have learned that it is easy to reach a burn-out state, and I'm slow to pull out of that state. So, I am learning to take better care of myself because no one else can do that for me. The result is a more enriched life with increased quality and meaning.

Goal setting is just the first step. Once I've set my goal, I break it into pieces and then decide how I'm going to get at that goal. I started by concentrating on a strong area first. For me, it was exercise. Then it was easier to add some of the other changes in lifestyle that hadn't been important to me in the past.

One friend told me, "I'm better at dealing with life than I used to be. I'm more at peace with myself now than I've ever been in my life. It's because of a strong spiritual foundation and because of my consistency in living by these principles."

Other clients, associates, and friends have told me about good attitudes that are related to their lifestyle changes:

"I enjoy my life more."

"I have more energy than I thought possible. I don't feel old and tired after work anymore. I'm raring to go!"

"I'm more productive now, and my co-workers are noticing."

"My career goals seem within reach these days."
"I actually feel like my life has more purpose."
"I feel ten years younger."

You're Never Too Old (or Too Young)

It's never too late or too early to excel. Mary Lou Retton, at age sixteen and weighing ninety-two pounds, was the first American to win an Olympic Gold medal in the all-around gymnastics.

Goethe wrote *Faust* when he was eighty years old.

Grandma Moses started painting when she was sixty-seven and produced 25 percent of her 1500 paintings after she turned one hundred.

George Bernard Shaw broke his leg when he was ninety-six. He fell out of a tree he was pruning!

During the 1984 Olympics, Carlos Lopez, supposedly over-the-hill, won the men's twenty-six-mile marathon at age thirty-seven.

Whatever stage of life you're in now, there's time to become more, to do more, and to be your best. Be patient with yourself as you begin this new journey of responsibility and discipline.

"There are no easy answers to coping with the stress of life," said world-renowned biologist, Dr. Hans Selye, who pioneered the research in what we today call the stress syndrome. "It takes years to learn. I've only had seventy-two years so far. Maybe with time, I'll learn to do better."

You may find that, like me, you're not perfect at managing the stress (demands) in your life—but you're good and getting better. We *are* winning because we're consistently doing our best.

The Disciplined Lifestyle

Four key words that relate to your new disciplined lifestyle are *compulsive, consistent, focus,* and *discipline.*

The first, however, is meant to remind you that it is important *not* to be *compulsive* about your progress.

Second, give attention to the *consistency* of your progress rather than the discrepancy between where you are and where you'd like to be.

Third, develop the ability to put on blinders and *focus* on what you want to improve.

Finally, start to learn the *discipline* it takes to stick with it.

Remember, a program of improvement is a slow process that requires patience. It is a brick-by-brick building process that has within the plans a stronger foundation and structure for a healthier, happier, and more productive life. Guard against your own natural impatience. Most of us have a tendency to be too hard on ourselves.

Like any pianist, singer, writer, typist, teacher, actor, or golfer, we get better at anything we want to do by patiently practicing *correctly*. We need to discipline ourselves to practice consistently and patiently until we see the results we desire.

Let me summarize with the 3 D's:

Desire—your goal or objective.

Discipline—consistently and patiently thinking, planning, and working toward your desire.

Delight—the feeling, experience, and excitement of achieving your desire.

Taking Care of Yourself

At one of my seminars a cynic responded to my talk with a dismal, "Life is a giant lottery. It doesn't matter what I do." My response? "Perhaps, but, regardless, you have to be present to win."

Jimmy Durante summed it up nicely: "If I'd known I was gonna live this long, I wooda taken better care of myself."

Centenarian Severo Santiago told us, "Life is sweet when you know how to live it; otherwise it can be very bitter."

Let life be sweet for you.

Taking care of yourself does make a difference.

You cannot guarantee how much difference, but you can closely predict it. On the other hand, you can also closely predict the results you'll experience if you choose *not* to take care of yourself. If we don't take time to be healthy (mentally, physically, and spiritually), we will *have* to take time to be sick.

Here is another way of saying it: People too busy to take care of their health eventually become too busy taking care of their health to do anything else. Although health does not insure success and happiness, they are short-lived without it.

Like the ostrich, we will, at times, stick our heads in the sand and ignore the realities and responsibilities of preparing to win, becoming our best, and doing our best. Ignoring those responsibilities and realities, however, will do little, if anything, to help us achieve what we most desire.

As my friend and mentor Christopher J. Hegarty put it, "Not everything that is faced can be changed, but nothing can be changed until faced."

Who's Going to Take Care of You?

Fred was anxiously looking out his farmhouse window at the rising river. It had been raining for several days—the water was already three inches deep in the yard—and there was no end in sight.

Just then the sheriff drove up in his Jeep and offered to take Fred to higher ground. Fred assured the sheriff that he'd be okay and that the Lord would take care of him.

Several minutes after the sheriff left, the water came up over the river bank and flooded the first floor, forcing Fred upstairs.

A couple of hours later, the sheriff came by in a boat loaded with some of Fred's neighbors. Again, Fred assured the sheriff that the Lord would watch out for him.

Within the next hour the rising water forced Fred to the roof. Again, the sheriff came to the rescue in the county helicopter. For the third time Fred replied that he wasn't leaving the farm and that the Lord would take care of him.

Soon after the sheriff left, the raging river rose above the house and swept Fred away.

In the next scene we see Fred talking to the Lord. "Lord, I don't understand why I'm here. I've been a godly man all my life. I've worked hard to be successful, and I was going to be married in a few weeks. The best years of my life, everything I've worked for is gone. In Joshua 1:5 You tell us, 'I will never fail you or forsake you.' It ain't fair. I really believed You'd take care of me."

The Lord replied, "Son, I tried. I really tried. I sent you a Jeep, a boat, and a helicopter."

I sincerely hope that the ideas, strategies, and techniques contained in this book will be of more help to you than the Jeep, boat, and helicopter were to Fred.

I also hope that this book has helped you become slightly anxious about what you are currently doing for yourself and others. And, lastly, I hope you have become a bit more optimistic about what you *can* do for yourself and others.

To begin this process, ask yourself, How much can I enjoy play, worship, work, and love? How can I help others enjoy play, worship, work, and love? The person who takes charge of his life realizes that total health and successful living find poor nourishment in the soil of complacency.

Living With Purpose

A Spanish philosopher observed that at the moment of our birth those who love us are joyous and smiling, while we come in crying. He suggested that if we can live our lives so that at the moment of death our loved ones are crying and we are joyous and smiling, our purpose will have been fulfilled.

The great educator Horace Mann said, "Be ashamed to die until you have won some victory for humanity." You and I will be honored and remembered not for what we received in life but for what we gave. And the greatest gift we have to give, to ourselves and to others, is the way we live each day.

You and I can prepare for a successful life by responsibly avoiding what hinders us and by responsibly utilizing what helps us fulfill the purpose for which God created us. We have no control over how much or how little ability we've got. God gives it to us, much or little. We *do* have control, though, over what we do with it.

Whatever your station, your loves, or your work, create a lifestyle you can live with. By consistently doing your best to realize God's full potential for you and helping others do the same, you'll enjoy a satisfaction that is rarely found in this life.

Whole Person Health Insurance Policy

We, the *Self Insurance Company,* will pay the insured the benefits of health, peace of mind, purposeful work, meaningful relationships, and financial security. These benefits are subject only to the provisions, limitations, and suggestions listed below.

Insured _____

Premium: Discipline

Premium Due: Daily

Consistently:
- Manage stress productively
- Develop positive attitudes and emotions
- Set aside time to be alone daily
- Develop and nurture a positive support network
- Develop personal and professional skills
- Put the grizzly bears of life in perspective
- Get moderate exercise three to five times per week
- Avoid tobacco use and polluted air
- Stay within 20 percent of recommended weight
- Eat a light, nutritious breakfast
- Avoid between-meal junk foods
- Develop a natural, energy-filled diet
- Avoid unnecessary drugs and medications
- Drink 48-64 ounces of unpolluted water daily
- Eliminate toxins, poisons, and waste products from the body
- Sleep six to eight hours a night
- Maintain a balance between play, work, worship, and love

Cancellation:
If you are not satisfied with this policy for any reason, you may cancel automatically by discontinuing your premium (defaulting on discipline).

Renewal:
Your policy will automatically be reinstated upon payment of your premium, which will always remain the same.

I, the undersigned, do understand the importance of consistently being responsible for my own physical, mental, and spiritual health. I further understand that taking care of myself is the best health insurance there is.

Signature of Insured _____
Date _____

For copies of this policy suitable for framing, send $3.00 to Turning Point Products, 640 S. Bear Claw, Prescott, AZ 86301. Quantity discounts are available.

Appendix
Relaxers & Flexercises
& Extendercises

Relaxers

Neck Roll

You've probably tried this already. But be prepared to use this exercise more often than you do now. It can help relieve tension in almost any situation.

Lower your chin to your chest and *slowly* roll your head in one direction, then the other. This is a natural and pleasant way to relieve the tension that builds in your neck, one of the most common places for tension to settle.

Flexercises

Flexercise 1

This first flexercise will:

- Reduce the pressure on the rear part of the lumbar disks
- Relax stretched muscles and ligaments
- Tone and strengthen abdominal muscles
- Tone and strengthen the muscles of the buttocks

1. Lie on your back with your knees bent and your feet flat on the floor (or bed). Place your hands under the small of your back.

2. Gently push your lower back down to the floor, squeezing your hands. Hold for six to eight seconds. Gradually increase the intensity of the downward pressure throughout the six to eight seconds.

3. Relax a few seconds. Repeat the flexercise three to four times.

4. Place your hands on your hips.

5. Gently try to raise your hips upward while applying pressure downward with your hands. Gradually increase the intensity of the upward pressure throughout the six to eight seconds.

6. Relax a few seconds. Repeat three to four times.

Flexercise 2

You will find that this flexercise:

- Strengthens abdominal muscles
- Provides support to a weak back
- Reduces pressure on the spinal disks
- Strengthens the lower back muscles
- Helps support and protect the organs in the abdominal pelvic area (stomach, spleen, liver, sex organs, bladder, and gall bladder)
- Helps insure that these organs function properly
- Helps prevent lower back pain
- Promotes regular bowel movement
- Enhances proper breathing
- Helps the body be prepared for childbirth

1. Lie on your back with your knees bent and your feet flat on the floor. Do not anchor your toes under any object or piece of furniture; this will diminish much of the value of the flexercise.

2. With your hands clasped behind your head, and your elbows touching the floor, slowly raise your upper body only until the lower back begins to rise off the floor. Pause.

3. Slowly lower the upper body to the floor. Repeat until you feel a slight straining or burning in the muscles of the abdomen. Be patient and *gradually* build to at least fifty of these flexercises each day.

Flexercise 3—The Instant Energizer

This flexercise:

- Improves blood circulation to the upper body and head
- Increases oxygen flow to the upper body and brain
- Releases tension in the muscles of the upper back, shoulder blades, and shoulders
- Stretches the legs
- Improves your energy level
- Improves creativity
- Improves problem-solving abilities
- Improves overall mental productivity

1. Stand in a comfortable upright position with your feet about shoulder-width apart. (You can also be sitting.)

2. Clasp your hands behind your lower back, stretch your arms, and roll your shoulders around.

3. Slightly bending your knees, slowly bend forward at the waist until your eyes are level with your knees.

4. Gently raise your hands and arms above your head and back in a circle like a windmill. Remain in this forward flexed position until you slowly complete twenty-five to fifty continuous circles with your arms. Gradually increase this to somewhere between fifty and 300.

5. Keeping your eyes open, take a slow deep breath through your nose as you slowly rise to your starting position. Repeat this exercise anytime you need a break or a little "instant energy."

Extendercises

These can be done while lying on your stomach or back, sitting or standing. Extendercises:
- Promote energy flow via the thirty-one pairs of spinal nerves in your vertebrae and the two gangliated chains of the sympathetic nerves on each side of the spinal column
- Gently stretch the ligaments of the spinal column
- Place gentle traction on the spinal column, promoting flexibility and elasticity
- Help correct deviations of the spine
- Relieve pressure and improve circulation to the intervertebral disks
- Develop elasticity of the lungs and expand the chest
- Stretch the heart and lungs and expand the chest
- Stretch and strengthen lower back muscles
- Strengthen and tone the muscles of the neck and shoulders
- Reduce lower back pain

Stomach Extendercise 1

1. Lie face down on your stomach with your feet nearly together and your forehead resting on the floor or bed. Put your hands palm down under the lower part of your neck with the longest fingers nearly touching each other.

2. Slowly and gently begin to raise your head and chest off the floor. Do this for five to ten seconds without the aid of your hands and arms.

3. Continue the gentle up and backward extension of your head and chest by slowly extending your arms. Your hips should not rise off the floor.

4. While in this extended position, slowly and gently look over your left and right shoulders alternately. This extended position and the rotation of your head should last ten to fifteen seconds.

5. Slowly and gently lower your chest and forehead to the floor and relax. Repeat two to three times, once or twice a day.

Back Extendercise 2

1. Sit on the edge of your bed with both feet on the floor.
2. Index a pillow against and across your buttocks.
3. Lie back on the bed with your hands above your head and relax for several minutes.

Note: This extendercise is a little less stretching or extending than Extendercise 1, but it is generally a little more relaxing.

Sitting Extendercise 3

1. Sit in a comfortable upright position in a chair.
2. Clasp your hands behind your head.
3. Keep your elbow parallel with your chest while slowly and gently stretching backward. Hold this position for ten to twenty seconds while slowly turning and stretching your upper body to the left and right.
4. Slowly return to the beginning position and relax. Repeat two to three times per hour when sitting.

Note: You may do this same extendercise standing up. *Bend your knees* slightly and be careful not to go over backwards!

Standing Extendercise 4

1. Stand comfortably upright two to three feet from and facing a wall. Your feet should be spread apart approximately shoulder width.
2. Leaning forward, extend your palms chest-high to the wall, fingers pointing toward and nearly touching each other.
3. With your arms slightly bent, slowly let your hips move toward the wall as you gently and slowly extend your neck

and shoulders backward. Hold this position for ten to twenty seconds while alternately looking over your right and left shoulders.

4. Slowly return to position one. Relax a few seconds and repeat. This is a good substitute when you are unable to hang by your hands. It can be done several times each day.

Upward Hanging Extendercise 5

1. Install a bar that will safely suspend and support the weight of your body.

2. Hold the bar so that the back of your hands are facing you.

3. While holding the bar with your hands, relax your body from the neck down. If you need to bend your knees to hang freely, put your feet behind you with the top of your toes resting on the floor and your heels pointing up.

Now imagine that your legs are gone from the knee down, and relax. It may help to let the body swing slightly and permit your head and chin to rock gently. The slight swinging enhances your ability to relax and therefore heightens the therapeutic effect. This extendercise can be done for twenty to thirty seconds several times each day.

I have installed bars across a door in my home and in my office. They are priceless. When traveling, I put a towel across the top of the hotel bathroom door for hanging. Wherever you are, invent a way to do this healthful extendercise (carefully).

The Inverted Extension

This exercise has the same positive effects as extendercises 1 through 5, plus it:
- Causes additional blood circulation in the neck area (rejuvenates the parathyroid and thyroid glands, which regulate body weight and metabolism)

- Promotes venous drainage of the legs, which benefits varicose veins, especially
- Provides additional blood circulation and oxygen to the head, improving the energy level, creativity, problem-solving ability, and overall productivity
- Helps balance the negative gravitational influence imposed on all bones, organs, and glands, thus helping to reduce premature degeneration and aging

The inverted extension offers the maximum decompression and elongation. You will need to purchase the bar described above as well as special boots designed specifically for the bar and inverted extension. The boots strap to your ankles in a way similar to ski boots. The most common style has a U hook on the front of each boot that hooks onto the hanging bar.

For those who prefer an easier and, in some ways, safer method of inverted extendercise, inversion swing systems are available for purchase. The system enables you to get into it standing up. By gently leaning back, you can slowly roll into an inverted position. When you want to go upright, it is balanced so that all you need do is extend your hands and arms toward your feet to be slowly rotated into an upright position.

I recommend that you purchase a bar rather than try to make your own. Safety during these extendercises should be your main concern. Most athletic supply stores carry them or can get them. Many facilities also permit you to try them before you buy.

Anytime you practice the inversion exercises, you'll feel the beneficial effects. I've found, however, that the best results occur after exercising (golf, tennis, jogging, etc.) and just before bedtime. Inversion is good after exercising because of the need for decompression and because the body is warm. It will be more flexible, and you'll find it easier to relax. At bedtime, inversion may help you balance from a day spent in an upright position. It also helps you cycle down, compose yourself, and relax.

A small percentage of people should not practice the inverted extension posture. By all means, consult your doctor and make sure that it is safe for you. When approached with caution and respect, this inverted posture can produce substantial health benefits.

About the Author

Ron L. Fronk was born and lived in Harvey, North Dakota, until age nineteen when he moved to Seattle, Washington, and went to work for the Boeing Aircraft Company. His next career started three years later when he became a professional flight instructor. He still holds an Airline Transport Pilot license.

In 1969, Ron began attending college part-time. Four colleges and twelve years later, he earned his Master's degree in psychology and his Doctorate in Wholistic Health Science from Columbia Pacific University in San Rafael, California.

Ron became a leading salesman and sales manager with two national sales organizatons. During one period of his sales career, he lived in thirteen different cities in two years. In 1975, he founded Learning Programs of America, a training and consulting firm now based in Prescott, Arizona.

For the past twelve years, Ron has been a professional speaker, entrepreneur, and author. As a speaker, he has addressed audiences primarily on lifestyle management topics. He is a published author of audio and video learning programs, training materials, numerous articles, and a unique self-assessing lifestyle appraisal.

Ron became interested in the differences between the personal characteristics and behavior of highly productive individuals who stay healthy and those who do not. His personal quest for maximum productivity while maintaining mental, physical, and spiritual health led him to write this book.

In November, 1977, Ron became a Christian by receiving Jesus Christ as his Lord and Savior. He is a lifetime member of the Full Gospel Businessmen's Fellowship International, a member of Fellowship of Companies For Christ International, and attends the Word of Life Assembly in Prescott, Arizona, with his wife Susan, stepchildren Jason and Molly, and daughter Kassandra.

He is the president and founder of *Voice For Need,* a non-profit organization serving the needs of the hungry, homeless, and illiterate in America.

What readers of
Creating a Lifestyle You Can Live With
are saying:

"Ron, Several days ago I wrote and thanked you for sending me your book. After starting to read it, I couldn't put it down.

"This book is filled with ideas and strategies for anyone committed to quality lifestyle. It's right on target, and I highly recommend it."

Nido R. Quebin
Chairman, Creative Services Inc.
Past President, National Speakers' Association

"After having read literally hundreds of self-help books, I know only a very strong work will hold my interest. I read your book from cover to cover. *Creating a Lifestyle You Can Live With* ranks among the top ten books that have had a significant impact on my life."

Richard D. Meiss, Vice President
Carlson Learning Company

"Refreshingly simple solutions for today's difficult lifestyle questions. Makes me want to 'take charge' of my life."

Patricia Fripp
Past President, National Speakers' Association
Author of Get What You Want

"Ron, I particularly admire the courage I see in your willingness to discuss unexciting subjects—like hurry, noise, and fat—as well as deeply personal subjects like God and love.

"In addition to drawing from your well-informed background and writing with a skillfully comfortable style, you have also dug deep within yourself to give us something very real and very personal."

Richard Crews, M.D.
President, Columbia Pacific University

"If you are truly interested in making a life as well as a living, Ron's book is a must for your library."

Christopher J. Hegarty, Ph.D.
President, C. J. Hegarty Company
Author of How to Manage Your Boss

"A spendid book. It will help many live longer, richer, and fuller lives."

Bob R. Conklin
Chairman of the Board, Conklin Company
Author of How to Get People to Do Things

"I thoroughly enjoyed your book. My wife is reading it now, and I'm going to share it with my parents when she is finished."

Denis J. LaComb
President, Sharden Productions, Inc.

"A common sense approach that can benefit anyone interested in living life to the fullest."

James E. Melton, Ph.D.
President, The Melton Corporation
Author of Your Right to Fly

"*Creating a Lifestyle You Can Live With* gives the simplest rules for living a healthy, happy, prosperous, and long life. If I'll just do what you tell me, I've got it made."

Robert H. Henry
Past President, National Speakers' Association
President, Henry Associates, Inc.

"Success is a journey—*not* a destination. Your book addresses lifestyle issues relevant to that journey. It is a storehouse of practical information and ideas that promote the quality of living we aspire to."

Cavett Robert
Chairman Emeritus
National Speakers' Association.

"*Creating a Lifestyle You Can Live With* is beautiful to behold in the mind, heart, and soul—and wonderful to hold in my hands. It makes me proud to be your friend."

Layne Longfellow, Ph.D.
President, Lecture Theatre Inc.

Product List

The Lifestyle Management System

Living To Win
This eight cassette audiolearning series presents numerous ideas and practical techniques for achieving high level health and productivity. It includes a study guide and the *Winning Lifestyles Appraisal*.

Living To Win Study Guide
Outlines and enhances the *Living To Win* cassettes and shows how the cassettes and the *Winning Lifestyles Appraisal* complement each other.

Winning Lifestyles Appraisal
Helps you evaluate thirteen different wellness areas and gives immediate feedback and recommendations for improvement.

Productive Relaxation
This four cassette audioleaning series gives techniques for unwinding, relaxing, and revitalizing via eight different relaxation sessions.

For information regarding speaking engagements or to purchase any of Ron's audiolearning series and study guides, write or call:

Susan J. Murphy, Marketing Vice President
Turning Point Products
640 South Bear Claw
Prescott, Arizona 86301
(602) 778-1733